HOW TO RUN
AN OFFICE

HOW TO RUN
AN OFFICE

Jennifer Rowley

KOGAN PAGE

First published in 1991

Kogan Page Limited
120 Pentonville Road
London N1 9JN

© Jennifer Rowley 1991

British Library Cataloguing in Publication Data

A CIP record for this book is available from the British Library.

ISBN 0-7494-0186-9

Printed and bound in Great Britain by
Biddles Ltd, Guildford and King's Lynn

Contents

Introduction

Time and money are the two major factors governing decisions concerning offices and office systems. This book assumes that the manager of the small business wishes to establish an effective office that is at the same time economical in terms of time and money. The options explored will enable the entrepreneur to build a firm foundation for the extension and development of office services in support of the growing business.

There are many books on office administration and practice, but few on office management. This book is addressed to managers rather than secretarial and administrative staff. A very experienced professional or business person may never have had any formal introduction to office practice. In a large organisation, it is easy to take office services for granted, but at the outset of a small business, setting up an office can be a daunting and unfamiliar task. This book starts at the beginning and makes recommendations for basic office configurations and systems, as well as exploring the requirements of the better established small business. It includes key aspects of such subjects as bookkeeping, office practice, office buildings, communications and the electronic office. All these topics can be studied in greater depth when the manager needs to know more.

1

The Office and its Environment

Why do I need an office? What does an office do?

Office work is secondary to the principal activities of the organisation, whether the business is involved in manufacturing or providing a service. Entrepreneurs start out in business to do what they are good at. Slowly, as a business grows, so will the associated paperwork, until eventually the business person can no longer put off the evil day when the office and its environment, practices, procedures and objectives have to be dealt with. At this point, the business person may be forced to consider the benefits of a well-organised office. It is more satisfactory and, in the long run, easier to establish appropriate office accommodation and office practices during the start-up phase of the business.

What should an office do? Since it is complementary to the main business activities, the precise nature of office work will depend on the nature of the business. Without an office, no materials can be ordered, no bills or wages paid, no invoices sent or payments collected, and no returns submitted. Clearly, the office is central to the operation of the business.

Larger businesses often boast a series of specialist offices supporting departments such as purchasing, production, administration, marketing, research, personnel and finance. All these sections are intended to fulfil the common objectives of an office:

1. *To receive information* of all kinds, from a wide range of sources, in a variety of different forms, and via different channels of communication. Channels of communication include: the written word, the telephone, word of mouth, facsimile transmission, telex, electronic mail and others.

2. *To record information* through the establishment and maintenance of appropriate information storage and retrieval systems, including paper filing systems and computer databases. Confidentiality is often an important issue.

3. *To prepare and arrange information* so that it is available in the most convenient form for future use. Information may be assembled, calculated, summarised, classified, interpreted, edited or duplicated.

4. *To communicate information* to those who need it, both within the organisation and outside, with a particular emphasis on customers or clients. The channels of communication available are the same as those for receiving information.

5. *To safeguard assets* or to account for all of the assets of the organisation and to draw attention to any irregularities. Central to this function is the record-keeping associated with the organisation's financial interests, and subsidiary roles may include the monitoring and recording of capital equipment and the reporting of bad debts.

These functions are common to all offices in any business. In the larger organisation, there may be separate office, secretarial or administrative departments; however, the small business person may need to perform some or all of these functions himself. The small business person must establish an effective and efficient office, so that office work does not detract from the achievement of the business's primary objectives.

In planning an office, it is helpful to view individual offices in terms of the kinds of service that they render. Key services are:

1. Secretarial support, including typing, shorthand, audio and word processing
2. Maintenance of records, as in filing and indexing
3. Distribution of incoming mail

4. Collection and despatch of outgoing mail
5. Control of stationery
6. Reception of visitors
7. Operation of switchboard and receipt of telephone messages
8. Duplicating and copying of documents.

Office management

Most of the office functions identified in the previous section can be executed by secretarial or administrative staff. There is therefore a temptation to appoint appropriate staff to tackle these tasks and then to abdicate responsibility. Unfortunately, to operate effectively and efficiently, an office needs to be managed. Responsibility for some aspects of office management can indeed be left to suitably experienced office staff, but the business person needs to monitor office operation to ensure that it supports the main objectives of the business.

Office management must be exercised in respect of the following areas:

1. *Purpose of the office*, particularly the identification of purpose and changes to meet changing conditions and the establishment of priorities.
2. *Organisation of the office*, with an emphasis on staffing and the profiles of staff responsibilities.
3. *Procedures and systems*, or how things are done in the office.
4. *Personnel issues*, such as recruitment, induction, training, working conditions, promotion, appraisal and dismissal.
5. *Environment*, such as the office building, furniture, lighting and heating, and other factors that influence working conditions.
6. *Equipment*, its acquisition, maintenance and replacement.

These areas are explored in the main chapters of this book. In this chapter, we start by considering the management of the office environment.

Planning the office environment

An office environment should be planned, not just happen. The environment has an effect on the extent to which office tasks can be completed quickly, efficiently and comfortably.

Too many offices in both small and large organisations are just accidents of history, and it may seem unrealistic to expect the small business person to devote time and effort to office planning when the larger business muddles along with accommodation, furniture and equipment that was more appropriate 20 years ago. The small business cannot, however, afford to waste time or money through poor office provision. Office accommodation and facilities must be adequate for their purpose, as well as being cost-effective. Unnecessary expenditure on redundant space or glitzy furniture is as inappropriate as cramped accommodation, which may lead to dangerous working conditions, difficulty in locating papers or general physical discomfort.

Location

The first consideration in office planning is the premises.

The location of the office may already be determined by the location of the business or workshop. Indeed, some businesses will be run from home, in which case the office will also be home-based.

When there is some choice in the location of an office, options will fall somewhere between city centre, suburban or rural sites. Each potential location may have its inherent advantages and disadvantages. Important factors to consider in evaluating a location are:

1. The general quality of the environment, its aspect, view and atmosphere
2. Car parking facilities for staff and visitors
3. Rent and rates and other overheads
4. Staff availability, staff salaries and staff turnover in the neighbourhood of the office
5. Security of premises

6. Public transport facilities, including air, train and buses, as these might be used by staff and visitors
7. Shopping and entertaining (in particular eating) facilities in the neighbourhood
8. Proximity to other sites that need to be visited, including both customers and suppliers
9. Any financial incentives available from the government to encourage businesses to locate in assisted areas.

Finding premises

The search for premises involves exploring all possibilities. This will include discussing requirements with a development officer attached to the local authority, if one exists in your area, and registering needs with estate agents. It may be necessary to follow up adverts in the local press and/or place an advertisement yourself. It is worth asking around and examining any empty premises or premises displaying estate agents' boards.

If the search for office space generates a number of options, then a preliminary report from an architect on the match between outline requirements and the options could be commissioned. Once an option has been selected as a front runner, a feasibility study could be undertaken to assess the option in detail in terms of facilities and costs.

A structural survey is a necessity. This should disclose the fundamental construction of the premises, which may affect the way in which those premises can be used. A structural survey should examine:

- floors and floor loadings
- existing walls
- acoustics and sound transmission
- fire worthiness and escape
- surface finishes and interior decoration
- lighting, heating and ventilation
- plumbing and sanitation.

The basic construction of a building may influence the above characteristics, as well as the extent to which it can be modified to meet specific requirements. There are three basic types of construction:

1. Load-bearing walls of brick or masonry with timber framed and clad floors, found most commonly in buildings constructed prior to the late nineteenth century.
2. Load-bearing walls of brick or masonry with solid floors, found in buildings constructed from the 1840s onwards.
3. Reinforced concrete or structural steel framing with solid or semi-solid floors, as used in most modern multi-storey office buildings.

Another important aspect to investigate is the use to which other parts of the building are being put, as this may affect the quality of the working environment, or the image that the office projects to visitors.

The Health and Safety Executive (for your local branch see the phone book) must be notified if a building is to be used for business purposes for the first time. The Fire Prevention Officer at the local Fire Authority should also be notified. Both will visit the premises and offer helpful advice. Production, planning and building specialists are available through advisory agencies and should be consulted if their expertise might be valuable.

Office accommodation can be broadly grouped into three major categories:

1. *Off-the-shelf accommodation* in an existing building that has been designed for office use and therefore needs the minimum of modification. Such accommodation is likely to meet the requirements of the business whose only premises is an office, or the business whose office may be located separately from any workshop.
2. *Accommodation in an existing building*, with either basic services that can be easily altered and augmented as required, or few facilities and requiring complete conversion and the installation of new services. This option may allow the office and the workshop to be located on the same site.

15

3. *New office space*, either individually or in co-operation with other businesses.

A fourth option may be added: the office in the home. This is dealt with on pages 32–35.

Often, the choice is between a modern office that may offer high standards with regard to most of the criteria listed in Checklist 1.1, but may be lacking in character, and a conversion of an older building that exchanges convenience for character and atmosphere. However, remember that building work takes time, and that time may be critical for a new or rapidly expanding business.

Checklist 1.1 *Factors to consider in assessing office accommodation*

1. Restrictions on room sizes and flexibility with which office sizes can be modified to suit changing requirements.
2. Floor loadings. Paper is heavy. Floors must take the loads of filing cabinets and safes.
3. Sound transmission, especially footstep noise.
4. Fire worthiness and fire escape routes.
5. Ease of installation, maintenance and modification of service runs for electricity, telephone and water.
6. Heating characteristics.
7. Restrictions on floor surfaces.
8. Surface coverings such as decorations.
9. Access, such as entrances, lobbies, lifts, stairs etc.
10. Mechanical and electrical servicing.
11. Plumbing and sanitation.

Leasing or purchasing

Some small businesses with, say, up to 20 or 30 staff may consider purchasing their own premises. To do this, it will be necessary to locate appropriate capital and arrange loans. One way of embarking upon a purchase may be to share a building with other businesses of the same size. An advantage of purchasing property is that the repayment of borrowed capital plus interest continues at a more or less consistent level.

Many businesses rent office accommodation. Renting involves taking on some unavoidable liabilities, but others may be minimised. For example, it is normal to pay the landlord's legal costs as well as your own, and to pay the landlord's insurance premium on the building. The leases may include a clause relating to 'full repairing and insuring' – this is known as an FRI lease. This means that you are responsible for all insurances and repairs to the building. Thus, it is important to carefully inspect, document and photograph the existing condition of the building and to agree a schedule of condition with the landlord. A solicitor or chartered surveyor should be consulted, both in relation to the contents of a lease and as a protection against future problems. They can offer advice, if, for example, the floor develops woodworm during your lease or there is a change of landlord.

Rates

Rates will be payable. Any quoted rates have a tendency to be out of date. It is advisable to check the actual rates payable.

Planning permission

The change of use of any building for industrial or commercial purposes requires planning permission. Check that this has been applied for and granted specifically with regard to the particular class of business into which yours falls.

If a building has been used continuously for a particular kind of business since before 1965, it is assumed to have planning permission for that activity. However, this still needs to be checked with the planning department and the situation confirmed in writing. The planning department may ask for an Existing Use Certificate, a formal confirmation of use rights.

If you have to apply for planning permission, you will be notified of the decision six to eight weeks after the application. If planning permission is granted, it will be in one of the following forms:

1. *Full planning consent*, where the building and the land can

17

be used forever for the specified activities.

2. *Temporary planning consent*, where the building and the land can be used by anyone for the specified activities, but there is a time limit and consent will need to be renewed.

3. *Personal planning consent*, where only the named person may use the building and the land for the specified activities.

There will normally also be other conditions to the consent, relating to the type of work that can be done and the hours of operation. Other injunctions might cover the storage of items out of doors and car parking arrangements.

When it is necessary to apply for planning permission, it can be useful to attempt to communicate with the people who may influence the decision of the planning committee. A discussion with the planning officer, possibly including a visit to the site, can help to smooth the way, and will ensure that you have some advice. After appropriate consultation, forms may be completed accompanied by drawings. Copies of your application will be sent to the water, gas, electricity and roads authorities and to the town or parish council for their comments. When the application is considered at a planning committee meeting, you may attend, but you cannot participate.

When a planning application is unsuccessful, it may be possible to reapply using a different form of wording or with minor modifications. A covering letter should explain the changes. After either the first or second unsuccessful application, you may appeal to the Department of the Environment. Appeals may be by public hearing or by written submission. Since public hearings are expensive, the commonest option for small businesses is written submission. You fill in the appropriate forms, which are then sent to the council who replies with its views. An inspector will visit the site and give a decision a month or two later. Professional advice from a chartered surveyor, architect or solicitor may be helpful.

Office design

Location of departments

The first issue to be considered in office design at the macro-level is the layout of a series of offices. The 'location' of offices is concerned with the arrangement of offices inside a building. The small business is unlikely to merit a network of offices, so this topic will only be given brief mention.

The most important consideration with regard to location is that offices that work together should be located next to one another. Any central services such as mail, messenger or toilets should be sited centrally, and departments with heavy traffic should be close to the reception area.

Layout and space allocation

Office space requirements must be established in some detail. Important issues to explore are: the way in which work flows through the office, how people move about the office, and how frequently, and which people or equipment need private offices.

To investigate movement and work flow, it is necessary to look at how work is done. In a small office, the pattern of activities should be fairly simple, but a relationship diagram may still help to clarify the picture. A relationship diagram is based on records; kept over, say, a typical five-day week, of the movement of people and paper. Such an analysis of work flow in the office should culminate in a draft office layout plan.

Any proposed layout that might emerge from a relationship diagram needs to be modified to take into account a host of other factors, such as the need to group 'noisy' work together, allocating space for different kinds of office function, or to make a distinction between private and general areas. For example, in the typical office, space needs to be allocated for entrance and reception, secretarial work, executive offices, meeting rooms, lavatories and rest rooms, catering, cleaning, and storage, etc. If that sounds a lot to fit into the two-room office suite that your business can afford, it is, and you will need to exercise even greater skill to fit everything in satisfactorily. Each of the above areas deserves individual consideration since, after the initial establishment of your office, it may be a long time before you examine any of these areas again with anything other than complacent familiarity.

Entrance and reception

If you expect to receive visitors, especially potential customers, the reception area is important in influencing first impressions. The reception area is intended to receive visitors, to provide a security or vetting process, and to set the tone of the office by its appearance, atmosphere and efficiency. Even in a small office where the entrance leads directly into the working area, a barrier in the form of a counter or desk should be positioned, to offer security and give the visitor a place to pause, take stock, report and be welcomed.

Attention to detail is essential. Signposting from the street, a bell-push and letter-box are cheap but important. In the reception area, one or two comfortable chairs, perhaps a table and a pleasant atmosphere will be welcoming. Other possible facilities that you might consider providing are: a convenient telephone and a stand for wet coats and umbrellas. The reception area is also a good place to display promotional material such as catalogues, publicity displays and photographs.

Secretarial offices

A secretary will be involved in a wide range of different activities including typing and/or word processing, filing, use of the telephone, visiting and passing messages to other people, and co-ordinating and arranging administrative matters. The secretary therefore needs access to certain equipment. As a minimum, the secretary needs a large desk, a chair, a separate word-processing workstation or desk, storage space for immediate supplies of stationery and personal belongings, shelves for reference books and files, a pinboard for notices and calendars, and filing cabinets. All this equipment occupies space, but must be accessible. There must also be room for the secretary to move about even when desk drawers are open.

Executive offices

Executive office activities derive from the nature of the business and are less standardised than those typical of the secretarial office. These activities may include formal meetings with a number of visitors, more casual meetings with office colleagues, telephone calls, reading letters or documents, and referring to books or files. Where a lot of documents are handled, desk space may be a priority. The atmosphere may be a more prominent consideration for the office that is frequently used as a meeting place. Comfortable chairs and the positioning of desks and chairs to facilitate satisfactory working relationships need to be considered.

Meeting rooms

A meeting room may be something of a luxury, but such a room can be widely used for entertainment, dining, presentations, interviewing, and internal and external meetings. The layout of the meeting room is dominated by the meeting table. The style and size of the meeting normally conducted in the room should determine the size of the table. Rectangular tables are regarded as being appropriate for formal meetings, while circular tables are more comfortable for think-tank sessions. Tables that comprise a number of separate sections and can be built up into different shapes to suit the occasion have much to recommend them. Chairs need to be comfortable, firm and sufficiently capacious for prolonged meetings. The general atmosphere, including heating, lighting, ventilation and acoustics, should also be considered. Meeting rooms usually also need to be equipped with wall charts, flipcharts, blackboards, projection screens and even a television.

Lavatories and rest rooms

Good quality lavatories are appreciated by both staff and visitors, and it is worth making adequate investment in this support facility. Facilities need to be sufficient to accommodate peak periods of use, such as just before lunch or at the end of the day. The following level of provision is worth seeking:

21

WCs: 1–10 staff, 1 WC
        11–20 staff, 2 WCs
        20–30 staff, 3 WCs

Hand-basins: 1–5 staff, 1 basin
                6–15 staff, 2 basins
                16–30 staff, 3 basins

Finishes and fittings should be good quality, all pipework should be covered, wash-basins and lavatory pans should be easily cleaned, and there should be mirrors over the basins, good lighting, good ventilation, shelves, coat hooks, tamper-proof and robust towel, soap and toilet paper dispensers, and shaving points for men. A shower cubicle may be a welcome luxury.

Catering and cleaning
A small amount of space needs to be allocated for small-scale catering facilities. Tea and coffee-making facilities are almost essential. A vending machine eliminates the need for washing-up facilities. A small refrigerator can be used to store drinks, milk and lunch-time snacks.

Space for cleaning equipment such as brooms, vacuum cleaners, buckets, cleaning solutions and floor-cleaning equipment is necessary. A cupboard or small store-room, preferably with easy access to running water, is ideal. Shelves and hooks for equipment help to keep the store-room tidy.

Storage
Offices need to store:

- stationery prior to use
- documents and other records for reference
- books and other reference sources.

Even in a relatively small office, some materials may be stored centrally, with, for example, stationery for immediate use located close to the individual's work area. Any store for documents needs to be gently ventilated, absolutely dry and preferably unheated. Loading of floors and walls in store-rooms for documents needs to be carefully assessed.

Corridors
Corridors are purely functional. They need to be wide enough to allow people to pass and chat to others. Corridors can be made more interesting by imaginative lighting and colour, and small recesses with plants or pictures.

Other considerations
The office design must accommodate space for all the above requirements and types of office. There are also four other considerations that should influence the basic layout of the office:

1. *Fire escape*. Since the age, construction and location of a building may influence the optimum fire escape routes, expert advice should be sought from the local Fire Authority, and this advice should be followed. Fire escape routes must be kept clear of obstruction.
2. *Needs of the disabled*. If the needs of the disabled are considered at an early stage in office planning, they can be much more easily accommodated. Many businesses employ disabled staff and it is important that they should be able to work independently, safely and efficiently.
3. *Open offices*. Open offices are shared offices with a number of staff working in the same area. The choice between open and closed offices, and which staff and activities should be assigned to which, will need to be made early in the planning process. The best layout of desks is with desks parallel to or at a constant angle to the perimeter. Screens (or partition panels) can be used to divide an open office, but their effect on work flow needs to be considered. Open offices should not be planned as internal spaces; everyone should be able to see a view from a window. Special attention needs to be paid to noise levels, lighting, heating and ventilation.
4. *Private enclosed offices*. Private enclosed offices offer a quieter environment than the open office, but may hin-

der effective communication and work-flow. Private offices are more essential for people who are conducting confidential business, or for those who are likely to be unduly distracted in an open office. Some people simply like the comfort of their own office. No office should be smaller than 5.5 metres square.

Checklist 1.2 *Criteria to be applied in office layout*

1. Aim for simple work flow, where movement of people and paper is minimised.
2. Avoid obstructions on floor space.
3. Office equipment, stationery, supplies and reference materials should be close to those who use them.
4. Gangways wide enough to facilitate safe and quick movement should be available.
5. Detailed work needing light should be sited close to windows.
6. Noisy machines should be soundproofed and segregated into separate rooms or, failing segregation, partitioned.
7. The office environment should be comfortable and pleasant.
8. Electrical sockets should be conveniently located and accessible.

Heating, ventilation and lighting

Heating, ventilation and lighting make a major contribution to a comfortable office environment. Often, the facilities will already be determined in the building in which the office is located, and will be beyond the control of the business owner. Nevertheless, a brief overview should help to identify any particularly inadequate or inappropriate arrangements. Established heating and ventilation systems are difficult to modify, but lighting and electric power systems can be modified relatively easily to suit individual requirements.

Heating and ventilation

Heating and ventilation are closely linked. The quality of heating, irrespective of the method used, depends upon:

- the volume of air to be heated
- how quickly it will lose or gain heat through external walls or windows
- how much heat will be generated by people, lighting and equipment in the room
- how often the air will be changed by natural or forced ventilation.

It is difficult to design a system that will accommodate changes in the office environment, such as greater levels of lighting or more people. Also, heat from the sun in offices with many windows can be extremely difficult to regulate.

Building construction and heating methods are central to the effectiveness of the heating system.

Building construction
A solidly built building acts as a thermal reservoir. It is slow to warm up and slow to cool down. Conversely, a lighter, possibly prefabricated building will be more subject to changes in outside ambient temperatures.

Heating method
Three basic kinds of heating method are in use:

1. Radiant surfaces
2. Convection
3. Mechanically ducted air.

Each has its own advantages and disadvantages, and suitability for a given application, together with estimates of capital and running costs, must be considered.

According to the Offices, Shops and Railway Premises Act 1963, offices should reach a temperature of 16 °C within the first hour of work. Most office workers would, however, be happier at about 21 °C for sedentary work. Providing heating that is acceptable to all is no easy task. Individual preferences, temperature differentials within a building and the effect of sunlight all militate against an ideal heating system.

Ventilation and humidity need to be adequate for a comfortable working environment. Opening windows, and using extractor fans, air cleaning equipment and full-scale air conditioning systems are some of the options. Ventilation improves productivity (you can't go to sleep!) and helps to reduce the spread of disease and associated absences.

A dry atmosphere may be caused by central heating. This can be alleviated with a humidifier which expels moist air. Humidifiers also help to reduce the static electricity generated by certain synthetic materials, such as those in carpets.

Checklist 1.3 *Criteria for heating systems*

1. Flexibility relative to office layout changes
2. Ease of extension of system or units
3. Speed of response to temperature changes
4. Uniformity of vertical heat distribution
5. Uniformity of horizontal heat distribution
6. Freedom from dust staining
7. Quietness of system
8. Freedom from transmission of office noise
9. Economy in operation
10. Flexibility in terms of temperature control
11. Installation, running and maintenance costs
12. Space occupied by boilers, pipes and radiators
13. General appearance.

Lighting

Legislative guidelines require that lighting be 'suitable and sufficient'. This phrase is not easy to interpret although its intentions may be clear. Light intensity can be measured and compared in lux or lumens per square metre. Both light intensity and light quality must be considered. Light quality depends on a number of factors:

- the type of light source
- the design of the light fittings
- the background contrast
- the kinds of surface on to which the light falls and from which it is reflected.

Natural lighting is always to be preferred, but supplementary lighting will also be required. There are two basic options for office lighting: the light bulb or the fluorescent tube. Fluorescent tubes are widely used in office areas. Although they involve a greater capital outlay, they are cheaper to run and give even, shadowless lighting. Fluorescent tubes can be linked up in banks or rows, sometimes behind suspended ceilings to yield very even lighting.

Checklist 1.4 *Criteria for lighting systems*

1. Flexibility relative to office layout changes.
2. Ease of extension of system or units.
3. Even, continuous lighting.
4. Some variation in lighting levels to offer visual interest and relaxation.
5. Switching arrangements that support the reduction of lighting to areas when only one or two staff are working.
6. Easy maintenance, which is supported by the use of standard fittings.
7. Minimal glare. The light source should not be directly visible from the workstation. Shading devices should diffuse the light and tone it down to moderate brightness. Colour and texture of interior surfaces also need to be designed to minimise glare.

Internal decorations

Internal decorations include wall, partition, floor and ceiling surface finishes. The internal decorations should be chosen to project an image; that image might range from anonymity to self-advertising indulgence. The appropriate image depends on personal preference and the nature of the business.

Floor finishes need to be chosen with care since they are one of the most expensive interior elements, and one of the most heavily used. The most wear-resistant floor materials, such as wood, quarry tiles and flexible vinyl, tend to be noisy in use. Carpet has become increasingly popular, with carpet tiles offering flexibility for the smaller office.

Ceiling finishes are the prime reflectors and distributors of light. Ceilings may also provide fixing and support and concealment for services.

Walls and partitions are visually important, especially in a smaller office, where finishes can be used to provide a sense of space and continuity. Possible finishes include paint,' wallpaper, fabrics, plastics, leather, cork, timber and tiling. Practicality, with a few variations in materials and their colour and texture, is a good policy.

Checklist 1.5 *Criteria to be considered for internal decorations*

1. The proportions of the office space.
2. The shape and form of the accommodation.
3. The pattern, including the pattern of lighting, ceiling tiles and partitions.
4. Texture, as on carpets, curtains and ceiling tiles.
5. Colour needs to be co-ordinated across desk tops, floor coverings, walls and partition panels. Strong colours are best avoided in an office, although too much neutral grey or beige needs to be broken up by some warmer colours, possibly in non-working areas.
6. Basic construction of the office premises. For example, jointless terrazzo flooring cannot be laid on timber floor construction.
7. *Fire resistance*. The Building Regulations demand a certain degree of fire resistance for some materials used in the office. In addition to specifying the fire resistance of walls, there are stated levels of resistance to flame spread for all finishing materials used in fire escape routes. Materials that produce large quantities of smoke, such as polystyrene ceiling tiles, are also to be avoided because of the risk of suffocation.
8. *Technical installations*. There must be reasonable access to cables, pipes etc without damaging surface finishes.
9. *Wear resistance* is particularly important for flooring, but even walls are subject to abrasion especially at skirting board, hand and shoulder levels.
10. *Ease of cleaning, replacement and redecoration*. The frequency of redecoration can be reduced by appropriate

choice of finishes. Smooth, hard finishes collect less dust than textured finishes. Changes in office layout are likely to provoke calls for redecoration. Some walls can be panelled so that only part of any area needs redecoration. Suspended ceilings also reduce the wall area to be decorated.

11. *Acoustics*. Interior finishes have a profound effect on acoustics. Acoustics is not simply a matter of reducing noise, but is concerned with the balancing of noise from various sources. Unwanted noise should be absorbed at source if at all possible.

12. *Cost*. The most expensive finish is not necessarily the best, but clearly cost needs to be weighed with the other factors.

Windows and doors

Windows let light and air in while excluding the elements. Windows need to be designed so that air can be let in without producing draughts and letting rain in. Also blinds and curtains need to be considered.

Windows should fit well and double glazing reduces noise transmission through them. Grilles may need to be fixed over windows accessible to intruders which may represent a security risk.

Doors are subject to heavy use. Door furniture, such as handles, push and kick plates, should be matching. Finishes must be robust. If security is a consideration, the doors must be solid, with wired glass in any glass panel and strong locks. Fire regulations require glass panels for visibility in certain circumstances.

Office furniture

There is a temptation to accede to status symbolism when selecting office furniture. Economics, however, usually dictates that the most elaborate furniture is not an option. Office furniture includes: desks, chairs, meeting tables, storage cabinets and bookshelves. Co-ordination of office furniture creates a unified effect, and furniture should also be compatible with the wider office environment.

Some office units are specially designed for the home office. These units fold away into the space occupied by the typical domestic shelving unit. They comprise a bureau desk with pigeon holes for stationery etc, a second desk for typewriter or computer, various small drawer units for stationery, tall cabinets or cupboards with shelving for box files, and bookcase units.

Systems furniture is a concept of co-ordinated furniture components which are flexible. Systems furniture allows individual workstations to be assembled, with work surfaces at different heights, and different shelving arrangements. Workstations can be linked together in a number of different configurations. This flexibility is attractive to the small but growing business, as components can be rearranged at a later date.

Wire management is particularly necessary in open offices, but always presents a problem. Arrangements need to be made for keeping unsightly and unsafe wires out of the way. Systems furniture has special channels for wiring. With different furniture, other solutions must be sought.

The basic set-up for a small office is likely to include:

- a desk, or two or three small desk units
- a filing cabinet
- one or more chairs
- bookcases
- waste-paper baskets
- coat stands
- special computer tables and data storage facilities.

Chairs

The physical considerations for chairs are listed in Checklist 1.6. The long list demonstrates the importance of a correctly designed chair. Basic dimensions affect posture and ease of working. The recommendations in Checklist 1.6 are based on British Standard 3893:1965.

A survey of office chairs will reveal a wide range of choice in shape, size, materials and price. Chairs fit into one of three major categories: executive chairs, general office chairs and typist/secretarial chairs. Executive chairs may be steel framed, wooden or aluminium. Most have swivel or tilt action, and can be upholstered in leather, fabric or synthetic materials. General office chairs and typist chairs are mostly steel framed for strength. They usually swivel and have adjustable seat and backrest heights, and have fabric or synthetic coverings. Moulded polypropylene chairs are cheap and durable, and good value, but are not usually adjustable or upholstered.

Adjustable height is important if chairs are to be used by more than one person. Some chairs have plastic slides, castors or wheels. The effect of these on floor coverings needs to be taken into account. Arms on a chair are a mixed blessing, especially where they prevent the user from getting close enough to the desk. Weight might be significant if the chair is moved frequently, and stability is always necessary.

Desks

Like chairs, desks can be divided into those for the executive and those for the secretary. Desks can be built up from standard components in order to suit individual needs. If the desk has a frame, then storage units may be suspended beneath a work top. The stability of frames depends on their connection to the work top. A heavy typewriter can place a significant load on a desk, so desks for typists must be strong. Desk tops can be finished in many materials, including wood veneer, lino and melamine. Checklist 1.6 explores other aspects of desk design that should be considered.

Checklist 1.6 *Physical dimensions for chairs and desks*

Chairs
1. Seats should not be higher than the length of the lower leg plus heel (430 mm is an average and adjustability between 393 mm and 495 mm is preferred).
2. Seats should be slightly less deep from back to front than the distance from the sitter's back to the back of the calf

(380 mm maximum; 330 mm minimum) and should be padded.

3. The seat should not be too narrow (406 mm minimum).
4. The seat may slope downwards towards the back at an angle of about 3 degrees.
5. The arms, if any, should not be too close together (480 mm minimum).
6. The arms must be sufficiently high so as not to encourage hunching (215 mm from the seat).
7. The back rest should be curved both from top to bottom and from side to side, and it should be fairly long, sloping backwards at an angle of 95 to 105 degrees or adjustable. It should be shaped to allow the buttocks to project backwards beyond the effective depth of the seat and should be padded.
8. Short bar-shaped back rests should be at least 100 mm deep and should not catch the shoulder blade.
9. The back rest should support the lumbar region, or lower part of the back. Greater comfort is achieved if it also supports the upper middle back or thoracic region.
10. The back rest should not interfere with the elbows.

Desks
1. Desk height must not cause hunching of the shoulders (710 mm is the recommended height).
2. Desk width must be adequate (450 mm is an absolute minimum).
3. The underside of the desk must be sufficiently high to offer adequate knee clearance. Vertical clearance above a seat should be at least 230mm.
4. The minimum knee-hole width should be 585 mm.

Working from home

Many of the topics that are aired elsewhere in this chapter may seem like a dream on the far horizon if you are just starting out as a small business. Many businesses start by operating from the owner's home. In these circumstances, the office will also be home-based. Indeed, businesses that are primarily office-based, in that they centre on information processing, are often the most suitable for running from home. The remainder of this chapter encompasses a spectrum of office sizes, but many of the issues addressed are also relevant to the home-based office.

A separate room is definitely preferable for the home-based office. If this is not possible, a corner with working space, including space for a typewriter or microcomputer and storage of records, is essential. The home-based office should be a planned environment. Consideration should be given to layout and space requirements. Heating, ventilation and lighting need to be appropriate, and the internal decoration and furniture should be carefully selected.

The main attraction of working from home is that it avoids expenditure on rent, rates and fares. An additional benefit is that no time is wasted on travelling to and from work.

On the other hand, care and consideration are paramount when working from home. Strictly speaking, working from home without planning permission is not usually allowed; your lease should be checked as your landlord or building society etc may want to be notified. In practice, however, the rules are often broken and working from home will cause no problems unless it causes harm to someone whose interests the planning regulations protect. Essentially, small businesses will be closed down only if they are nuisances. Common sense dictates what constitutes a nuisance, and the wise business person will work quietly and ask visitors to park cars so that they do not cause an obstruction. Be careful with delivery vehicles, customer visits, obstructions, unsightly equipment, and noise or offensive smells.

Most people do not require planning permission when setting up an office in their own home. However, problems may arise. Advice should be sought if:

- the character and use of the building is no longer essentially residential
- the external appearance of the property is affected or access roads are altered
- an extension is to be built.

A booklet entitled 'A Step-by-Step Guide to Planning Permission for Small Businesses' is issued by the Department of the Environment, and should be available from your local authority.

Insurers should be informed that your home is being used for business, otherwise some exclusion clause may leave you uninsured. If it is being purchased on a mortgage, the firm that lends the money should be told. A solicitor can advise if anyone else needs to be notified.

Notices to display the name of the business do not require planning permission, provided they do not exceed specified sizes and weights. Another booklet issued by the Department of the Environment entitled 'Outdoor Advertising for Small Firms' gives advice.

Options for working from home

There are a number of options for allocating office space in the home. These include:

1. *Studies*. The study, as an integral room in the home is probably the best option, since it makes it possible to carry out both business and domestic activities, particularly with regard to opening the front door, answering the telephone and supervising the family. However, it is essential that the office door can be closed! Downstairs studies are preferable, since offices create dust and dirt, and access for visitors is better.
2. *Built-on extension*. Any kind of extension from a conservatory to a purpose-designed office may make an appropriate office, and will not intrude on other domestic uses of the home.
3. *Portakabin offices*. These offices can be set up in the garden and offer instant accommodation, possibly to cover the building or acquisition of other offices. Portakabins may be hired or purchased.
4. *Ancillary buildings* such as potting sheds, garages or garden sheds are often cheap solutions. They tend to be spartan and uncomfortable, with heating, lighting and access to the telephone being potential problems. If this is

the only option available, the associated inconveniences may have to be tolerated.

Access and reception for visitors

Access and reception arrangements for visitors need to be considered with the office at home. If visitors are infrequent, they may be received in the domestic lounge (although this puts extra pressure on cleanliness and tidiness). If visitors are numerous, a separate front door and reception area must be considered.

The tax position

Where a home is used partly for business, it is possible to agree with the Inland Revenue that some fraction of the household expenses be regarded as deductible. The snag with this arrangement is that capital gains tax may be due on a fraction of the home if it is sold at a later date. Accountants' advice should be sought on this issue.

Safety in the office

Apart from interested concern for oneself and staff, all organisations have a statutory obligation under the Health and Safety at Work etc Act 1974 to produce a health and safety document for publication or issue to employees. This document should describe the company rules, regulations and procedures in relation to safety practices. Specific factors that need to be considered with regard to safety in the office are listed in Checklist 1.7.

Checklist 1.7 *Factors to be considered in office safety*

1. The building and general layout, with particular attention to gangways, entrances, corridors, lifts and staircases.
2. Doors, and the need to keep fire doors closed.
3. Windows and their opening and closing.
4. Lighting.

5. Installation, maintenance and servicing of electrical appliances and other equipment.
6. Training in use of equipment and safety procedures. Staff and their manager must follow instructions on the use of equipment, and adhere to safety procedures.
7. Provision and maintenance of step-ladders and trolleys where necessary.
8. Warning notices on faulty equipment and potential hazards. Any faults in equipment should be reported immediately and attended to. Staff should not tamper with electrical equipment that is not functioning properly.
9. Wiring.
10. Correct storage of flammable liquids and other dangerous materials. Many correcting and cleaning fluids give off inflammable vapour, so tops should be replaced immediately.
11. Guards on equipment, especially guillotines.
12. No smoking where there is any danger of fire, such as store-rooms, and the use of ashtrays not waste-paper bins.
13. Do not lift heavy weights; use a trolley. Ensure that equipment is securely placed on desks.
14. Do not open the heavy top drawer of a filing cabinet without also opening the bottom drawer. An opened top-heavy filing cabinet is liable to topple over.
15. Be conscious of safety.

Security

Security covers both security of premises and equipment, and security of information.

Security is particularly likely to pose a problem for the small business in shared premises. Much office crime is committed by strangers just walking into an office block, picking something up and walking out with it. Unobtrusive security measures need to be introduced and everybody needs to be aware of the procedures in operation. Access to premises needs to be controlled and visitors should not be left unattended. Keys need to be under strict control, and equipment inventories need to be taken at frequent intervals.

Security of information involves careful control of any copies of confidential papers and password protection to computer files.

Summary

The office environment is a primary consideration in office design. First, it is necessary to locate premises, and then to allocate space for each of the functions of the office. Heating, ventilation and lighting also need attention, and finally furniture must be acquired.

2

Office Personnel

What do office staff do?

A large organisation often boasts a range of different types of secretarial, administrative and clerical posts. For example, posts may exist with all of the following job titles:

- office manager
- personal assistant
- senior secretary
- secretary
- junior secretary
- shorthand typist
- audio-typist
- copy-typist
- secretarial services supervisor
- word-processing supervisor
- clerk
- office junior
- receptionist
- telephonist.

The smaller organisation will need staff who can fulfil a number of the functions covered by this plethora of posts simultaneously. The extent of each of these jobs may be much more limited in the smaller organisation, since there will be fewer visitors, fewer telephone calls and fewer documents to process. Often, much less complex office systems can work satisfactorily. Office staff in the smaller organisation must be flexible, as well as willing and able to tackle a range of office functions.

Whether office operation is in the hands of secretarial staff or the small business manager, effective operation involves:

1. *Office management*, including decision-making associated with the office environment, office equipment and office procedures and practices, and the relationship between these and the organisation.
2. *Execution of office activities*, including text preparation, receiving visitors, taking or routing telephone calls, filing documents, booking appointments and keeping diaries.
3. *Supervision of office activities*, including ensuring that office practices and procedures are being followed, and supervising the training of new staff and the installation of new equipment.

In a one-person business, all these functions must be performed by the business owner/manager. Once the scale of office activities justifies the appointment of office staff, these specialists can focus more directly on office activities. Figure 2.1 shows some typical office staffing arrangements for a small business. Where only one office worker is employed, that person will take responsibility for the full range of office functions, unless some of these are retained by the owner/manager. With such a staffing configuration, the lone office worker can easily become isolated, being tied to a word processor and telephone in an office that has few visitors. It is important that the lone office worker be involved with the wider organisation. He must feel part of the business and be given the opportunity to identify with the objectives of the business. Receiving visitors can relieve an otherwise monotonous existence.

Once the organisation has grown to the stage where either Model C or Model D in Figure 2.1 is appropriate, the business will also be employing a number of production and marketing staff, and the allocation of secretarial support to such staff will also need to be considered.

Are office staff necessary?

While all small businesses need effective office management, a manager always needs to consider carefully whether there is sufficient work to justify the appointment of additional staff, and whether the business can support them. Staff are a com-

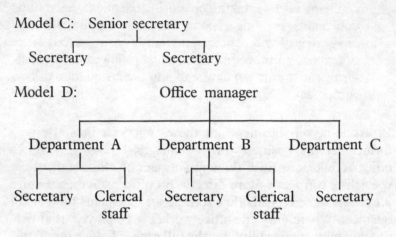

Figure 2.1 *Models for office staffing arrangements*

mitment and may represent a liability if business becomes slack or goes through a bad patch. In addition to salary and associated overheads, any member of staff incurs other extra expenditure. For each additional member of staff, a desk, chair, typewriter or word processor and storage units are basic requirements. Additional staff also occupy space, and this may be a particular problem in the home-based office.

Office staff should be employed to release management from office activities so that time can be employed in generating profits. Once office tasks start to interfere with the fulfilment of the main objectives of the business, it is time to seek assistance with office activities.

An assessment of the magnitude of office tasks should clarify whether full- or part-time staff need to be sought. Arrangements for working hours of part-time staff must suit the requirements of the business, but the more flexible the working hours offered, the more likely it is that a motivated and competent secretary will be available at a competitive salary. People who have taken early retirement, married people with family commitments and students are worth considering as part-time and/or short-term employees.

Freelance secretarial services are widely available and may be appropriate for the 'one-man band'. Such help may be useful to word process documents, deal with mailings, respond to routine enquiries for brochures and file documents. If freelance services are engaged, a clear relationship with the business should be established, whether it is on a fixed or casual basis. However, employee–employer relationships should be avoided to ensure immunity from PAYE deductions and NI contributions.

Freelance bookkeeping services are also available, but as long as the business is sufficiently small for the bookkeeping to absorb relatively little time, the owner/manager should consider doing the bookkeeping himself. Keeping close financial control is central to success of the business and doing the bookkeeping yourself makes sure that you are well informed about the financial health of the business. In the early days of a small business, make it a golden rule to sign every order and cheque yourself.

What to look for in a secretary

The appointment of the right staff in a small business can be crucial to the success of the business. Since the business will have relatively few staff, sometimes only two or three, a lot hangs on their performance. Office staff must have personal qualities that will help them to fit into the business and be able to display the initiative and independence often required. In assessing potential secretarial staff, the following should be investigated:

1. *General education.* A good general education is desirable, accompanied by a sound mastery of English. Some secretaries may have a degree, a Higher National Diploma in Business Studies (HND) or A levels. Such qualifications are useful for an office manager, or per-

41

sonal assistant, but secretaries with these qualifications may be rather expensive for the small business, except on a freelance basis.

2. *Secretarial skills*, such as typing, audio, shorthand, spelling, display, filing, reprography and telephone techniques. A reasonable shorthand speed is 100 words per minute, while a good typing speed is 50 words per minute.

3. *Business knowledge*. A general background in business administration and the operation of offices in support of various types of businesses. Such knowledge will often be acquired during previous work experience.

Recruitment and selection

Recruitment and selection is time-consuming and costly, and involves crucial decisions. Therefore, it is important to get it right the first time. The small business owner/manager is often inexperienced in staff recruitment and selection. Supplementary expertise can be acquired by engaging recruitment consultants, but these outsiders cannot be expected to have the same intuitive appreciation of the business's requirements as its owner/manager. Another way to ease the uncertainty associated with staff selection is to use agency staff on a temporary basis, and to take the opportunity to watch them on the job before making an offer of a permanent post. Although both of these strategies reduce the uncertainty in staff selection, they are likely to be more expensive in the short term than exercising your own judgement in the standard recruitment process.

Draw up a job description.

Job description

This will form the basis of your advertisement. Enquirers should be provided with details of the post in the form of a job description which should provide the following information about the post:

- job title
- salary

- location
- purpose of the job
- main duties and responsibilities
- specific duties
- position within the organisation's structure
- working environment
- training opportunities
- conditions of employment.

The job description needs to be supplemented by a job specification, which focuses on the knowledge, skills and attitudes that are required to be able to perform the job effectively.

Advertising

Advertising should aim to ensure that any vacancy is brought to the attention of as many potential candidates as possible. Usually, an advertisement in the appropriate local newspapers or specialist journals will be indicated. Other options include approaching office recruitment agencies, contacting local educational establishments or professional bodies, and trawling personal contacts. If the post is part time, local advertising in the narrowest sense will be particularly important.

Base your advertisement on the job description. Any advertisement should contain all of the following:

- job title
- details of the job
- necessary qualifications
- essential characteristics of the person sought (eg skills, experience, abilities)
- nature of the organisation's business
- location
- salary details and other significant or attractive aspects of the job (holidays, pension etc)
- how prospective candidates should apply
- closing date for applications.

Application forms and CVs

Small organisations are unlikely to have sufficient staff turnover to justify a tailor-made application form, so most applicants will be required to submit a curriculum vitae (CV), together with a covering letter. If there is a large number of applicants for a post, applicants must be short-listed on the basis of their written applications. The owner/manager can ascertain quite a lot from a written application. The presentation in terms of tidiness, layout and logical order may be a very good indicator of the calibre of potential office staff. However, content should be more important than presentation. The application should give basic information about the applicant, such as age, home address, travel distance to work, education, qualifications and previous experience. The motivated applicant should have taken the trouble to sell himself, and to explain both why he is interested in a particular post and how his previous experience equips him for the post. The written application can also provide an opportunity to monitor spelling and quality of business English. When drafting a short list, there are two basic questions that need to be asked:

1. Has this candidate the skills to do the job?
2. Will this candidate fit into the working environment and work effectively with other staff?

All applications should be acknowledged, whether or not they result in an interview.

References

Applicants should be asked to supply references, and references should be taken up. References are not guarantees, but it is useful to have someone else's opinion of the candidate, and they may help you to avoid a really disastrous appointment.

References may be taken up at different points in the application process. All references may be collected for all applications prior to short listing; alternatively, references may only be requested for short-listed candidates or may only be taken up when a conditional appointment has been made. Applicants should be told what will be done about their references. Some may request that referees should not be contacted unless a job offer has been made, subject to a satisfactory reference.

Referees should be sent job details and asked to comment on the applicant's suitability for the post, as well as answer more specific questions on the candidate's abilities, personality, integrity and health record.

Some applicants may present testimonials, but these should be treated with scepticism as it is difficult to check whether they are authentic. Testimonials testify to the character, integrity and professional competence of an individual, and are often supplied when someone leaves a post. If you are considering a testimonial, a telephone call may provide a check.

Interviews

Short-listed candidates should be called for an interview. For secretarial and similar posts, a short list of three to five applicants should be sufficient. Too long a short list is symptomatic of early indecision.

The interview is the main forum in which the employer can further determine the suitability of the candidate for the job, and the candidate can learn more about the vacancy. The interview is a two-way process, with both sides anxious to impress; the interviewee is selling himself, while the interviewer is selling a job. The outcome of an interview may be that the employer may or may not offer the job, and that the applicant may or may not accept any post offered.

Interviews are inevitably rather artificial social encounters upon which important decisions hang. Good organisation and planning of the interview can increase the effectiveness of the interchange.

Candidates need to be invited for interview, and informed of the date, time and venue for the interview, including any supplementary arrangements for preliminary talks, tours of the business or tests. Directions to the location of the interview, together with a contact person and a telephone number if there are problems, are important.

There are a number of possible strategies for organising a

series of interviews. All candidates may be interviewed on the same day, and possibly participate in preliminary group sessions, or interviewees may be called over a series of days. In the interests of effective comparison, and making an appointment before applicants find another job, interviews should be reasonably concentrated in time. Interviews may be conducted by one person, two or more together, or a series of people one after another. Formal interviews usually use an interview panel, but informal discussions may be more effective if the applicant talks to people one after another. Even in a small business, a second opinion may be welcome, and, if necessary, a consultant with experience of interviewing may be engaged to assist.

Adequate preparation starts with a mechanism for receiving candidates. Any staff involved in the interviewing process should be fully briefed with regard to times, their role and the background of the applicants. A comfortable interview room needs to be organised with suitable seating, heating and lighting, and no possibility of interruption.

Interviews should be well structured. If a panel is responsible for conducting an interview, the members of the panel should meet before the interview to agree the order of events and the role of each member. Employment legislation should be noted in framing questions. Particular attention should be paid to the provisions of the Equal Pay Act 1970, the Sex Discrimination Act 1975 and the Race Relations Act 1976.

The appointment

Once all interviews have been completed, it should be possible to make a decision concerning the most appropriate candidate for the job. Usually, one or more candidates will meet the selection criteria, but if none of the interviewees is suitable you should think again rather than making a hasty appointment. It is sometimes tempting, in desperation, to appoint the best of an unsuitable bunch; this is a recipe for disaster. If the interviewing process has been unsuccessful, it may be necessary to think again, and possibly to readvertise the post at a different salary, with different working conditions or elsewhere.

The offer of appointment may be made verbally in person, over the telephone, or in writing. Once the successful candidate has accepted the post (and not before), it is courteous to notify the unsuccessful candidates, and to thank them for their time and interest.

The first offer should be followed by a written letter of confirmation. This is usually accompanied by a document that outlines the terms and conditions of employment, or, possibly, the actual Contract of Employment. Employment legislation under the Employment Protection (Consolidation) Act 1978 requires that full-time employees should receive, within 13 weeks of starting work, details of the major items of the contract. Technically, a contract exists when an offer of employment is made and accepted; it is not necessary for a contract to be written for it to be binding. Nevertheless, a written contract is a better basis. Checklist 2.1 lists the topics that a Contract of Employment should encompass. The contract should be prepared in duplicate, with the applicant signing and returning one copy and retaining the other for personal reference.

There may also be other aspects of employment law that are relevant, even when there are only one or two employees. A handbook, such as *Croner's Reference Book for Employers*, can offer useful advice.

Checklist 2.1 *Items to be included in a written Contract of Employment*

1. Names of the parties
2. Job title
3. Outline duties
4. Commencement date
5. Rate of pay
6. Hours of work
7. Holiday arrangements
8. Sickness allowances and notification requirements
9. Periods of notice either side
10. Grievance procedures
11. Union membership arrangements
12. Disciplinary procedures

13. Rules appertaining to the work
14. Arrangements for terminating employment
15. Any special rights or conditions
16. Any rights to vary the contract.

Induction

All new employees need to be welcomed to the company and provided with basic information about the company, its activities, procedures and facilities, and what is expected of them. An induction programme of some kind is necessary to help new employees settle into an organisation. Checklist 2.2. lists typical topics that would be incorporated into an induction programme in a larger organisation. The small business owner/manager might use this checklist to select those topics that are appropriate.

Induction information can be imparted at a variety of levels of formality. Tours, talks and informal discussion may all be used. A staff handbook may be a useful reference tool, especially if there are frequent staff changes, within a small staff.

New staff also need the opportunity to become acquainted with other staff with whom they may be working.

Induction may include some job-specific training. For office staff, this is likely to involve learning about the business and its office systems.

Checklist 2.2 *Aspects to be covered by the induction programme*

1. Company background information
2. Organisational structure
3. Company development plans
4. Health and safety information
5. Salary arrangements
6. Employee profit-sharing schemes
7. Pension schemes information
8. Disturbance allowance provision
9. Sickness notification requirements and procedures
10. Holiday arrangements
11. Company rules and regulations

12. Company systems and procedures
13. Education and training facilities and provision
14. Appraisal schemes
15. Promotion procedures
16. Grievance procedures
17. Disciplinary procedures
18. Union matters
19. Medical services and first-aid facilities
20. Social and sports facilities and activities
21. Restaurant and canteen facilities.

Training

All organisations, however small, need to make the most of their staff. Appropriate training keeps staff up to date and helps them to reflect upon and improve working practices. The opportunity to attend training courses can also enhance job satisfaction and contribute to a feeling of being appreciated. In a small business, the training programme is likely to be modest, but a limited programme of two or three days a year per member of staff is a worthwhile investment that should lead to a more skilled and stable work-force.

There are many different kinds of training course available from a number of agencies. Courses cater for all levels of previous experience. Programmes are marketed by educational establishments, freelance training providers, professional and trade bodies, training organisations, and manufacturers and suppliers. Courses vary in length from one day upwards. Careful selection should ensure that training objectives are met.

Performance appraisal

Formal performance appraisal techniques are unlikely to be appropriate in a small organisation, but even there the owner/ manager needs to establish some simple appraisal procedures which support the monitoring of staff performance and impress on staff that their performance is important, and that their contribution has been noted.

Staff may be appraised in order to:

- collect data that allows the organisation's performance to be improved
- identify staff training and development needs
- motivate staff to improve their performance
- provide staff with an opportunity to discuss their career plans
- offer an opportunity to praise
- offer an opportunity to explore weaknesses in their work.

Appraisal may be conducted through an annual interview. A supervisor may prepare a written statement about the employee. This will be prepared with the aid of a checklist. Alternatively, staff may be asked to write an evaluation of their own performance, which can be used as a basis for an interview. The appraisal process needs to be worthwhile for both participants and must have identifiable outcomes. Typical outcomes are jointly agreed decisions, the elimination of problems, the introduction of changes and planning for training. Interviews are a useful part of the process in that they encourage communication and the exchange of views. All participants need to understand the objectives of appraisal and the structure of the interview.

Staff will be concerned with their future prospects. Salary reviews should be undertaken on a regular basis, say annually. Promotion prospects for office staff in a small business are not likely to be good, so the owner/manager must accept that, in time, staff with marketable skills will move on. If promotion prospects are limited, it is all the more important to ensure that employees have a satisfying and agreeable job. Office staff have skills that are easily transferable to another work environment, so the quality of the environment and the job are all the more crucial to a stable work-force.

Employment law

The first employee brings with him the need to observe relevant employment law. A summary of some of the key issues is offered in *Starting a Successful Small Business* (see page 154). Areas that may need to be considered include the following.

Employment protection and dismissal

In a company employing no more than 20 staff, the employee qualifies for protection from dismissal without good reason after two years' employment. Employees are further protected from dismissal on grounds of race, sex, pregnancy or trade union activity, irrespective of their length of service. An employee must have worked at least 16 hours per week for two years to be entitled to employment protection. If the company employs five people or less, a pregnant employee does not have the right to insist on reinstatement following the birth, if it is not reasonably practicable for her to return to employment. In larger companies, the pregnant employee has the right to reinstatement, subject to certain conditions being met.

On occasion, it will be necessary to dismiss staff. Admissible reasons for dismissal are redundancy, misconduct, incapacity for the work or some other sound reason such as strong personal incompatibility.

Industrial tribunals

If you are called upon to appear before an industrial tribunal because an employee feels he has been unfairly dismissed, the onus is on you as the employer to prove that you did dismiss the employee fairly. The employee has three months after leaving your employ to put a case in writing, and you are expected to put your view of the situation in return, with the support of your solicitor. An officer from ACAS will attempt to settle the matter, and should succeed. If the matter is not settled at this stage, the ACAS official will report to an industrial tribunal, at which both the employer and the ex-employee will be called upon to give evidence. Industrial tribunals can be expensive. Awards are high and the loser runs the risk of having costs awarded against him. Avoid circumstances that might lead to an industrial tribunal if at all possible, and if you do get involved, take advice on the strength of your case.

Disciplinary procedures

All organisations need disciplinary procedures which should

51

be applied consistently. Unacceptable conduct must be identified and monitored. If conduct is sufficiently bad to justify dismissal, a case needs to be built up and recorded in writing. There are three steps in normal disciplinary procedures:

1. *Verbal warning*, which is recorded on the employee's file.
2. *Written warning*, explaining that the behaviour could lead to dismissal.
3. *A letter of dismissal*, putting the reasons in writing, usually drafted with a solicitor's help.

Grievance procedures

A grievance procedure lays down the procedure for employees who wish to make a formal complaint to their employer. The grievance procedure is complementary to the disciplinary procedure. In large companies, the grievance procedure may be complex, involving several layers in the management hierarchy. In the small company, grievances are often dealt with by the owner/manager. Procedures should still retain an element of formality, and even though you may feel threatened by complaints, it will be counter-productive to ignore them. Listen, as you might learn something that you had overlooked. At the very least, the employee will have had an opportunity to let off steam and working relations should be improved. The interchange should ideally be resolved at a first meeting, but if it is necessary to pursue the matter further, a second meeting can be arranged in which both sides may take notes.

Summary

Office staff are important in supporting the small business. The owner/manager needs first to establish the requirement for office staff, and then to carefully select the appropriate staff. This chapter has briefly reviewed many of the facets of the recruitment and management of office staff.

3

Office Equipment and Supplies

Office equipment and supplies – some definitions

Office equipment comes in all shapes and forms. It encompasses a large number of individual items that are used to support the basic office functions of receiving, recording, preparing, arranging and communicating information. The scope of office equipment may be easily demonstated by examining the catalogues of some of the major office equipment suppliers. One such catalogue has the following sections:

- Desks and screens
- Chairs and metal storage
- Personal and office accessories
- Machines
- Conference and presentation aids
- Packaging, postroom and warehouse
- Computer supplies
- Archival storage and filing
- Office and secretarial supplies
- Writing and graphic supplies
- Books and pads
- Envelopes and paper.

This basic list may be amplified by examination of the contents of some of these sections. For example, the section on personal and office accessories includes plastic cutlery, refrigerators, clocks, brief-cases, planners, home-files, racks and waste bins. The section on machines is also wide ranging, encompassing fax machines, word processors, PCs, typewriters, copiers, calculators, cash registers, dictation equipment, letter folders and paper shredders.

Some of the items that might be regarded as office equipment are discussed elsewhere: furniture, including chairs, screens (partition panels) and desks, were covered in Chapter 1. Storage and filing systems are a central concern of Chapter 6, while the various components of computer systems are drawn together in Chapter 4. This chapter discusses the very assorted group of office equipment that is not considered elsewhere and briefly considers office supplies.

The distinction between office equipment and supplies needs to be made at an early stage.

Equipment constitutes the machines that facilitate office activities. These machines are hired or purchased once and thereafter are expected to give faithful service for a period. Typical examples of office equipment are typewriters, staplers, computers and dictating machines. The central issues in the management of office equipment are appropriate initial selection and satisfactory maintenance arrangements.

Supplies are items that support the operation of the office equipment and other office activities. Supplies, by their nature, are used once only and need to be replaced with another item of the same kind for the next time. Examples of supplies are paper, envelopes, staples and drawing pins. The specification of the supplies will sometimes be determined by the equipment with which they are to be used. The central concern in the management of supplies is the monitoring and, if possible, control of their rate of use, so that economic stock levels can be maintained.

Both equipment and supplies are essential to every office.

The next section deals with strategies for the acquisition of office equipment and the criteria to be applied. These general criteria are appropriate in the selection of all kinds of equipment, including those dealt with in other chapters, such as furniture and computer equipment.

What to look for in office equipment

Perusal of office equipment catalogues not only demonstrates the wide range of office equipment but also confirms suspicions that the acquisition of office equipment could, without any difficulty, consume rather too much of your hard-earned cash, or too large a proportion of a new business's capital. Only essential equipment should be acquired initially. However, as the business expands, so will the office activity, and office equipment needs should be reviewed from time to time to ensure that the equipment is adequate for the business. Any financial projections for a business should make some provision for expenditure on office equipment each year. Equipment needs to be replaced and updated from time to time. Different items of equipment have different life spans, so each item needs to be considered separately, and plans to replace expensive pieces of equipment need to be made in good time.

In a chapter on office equipment, there is a danger of sinking into a technical and routine rehearsal of the functions of the various items. This potential hazard is negotiated by viewing office equipment from the standpoint of the potential acquirer of the equipment. Questions that are paramount in the acquisition of equipment are:

1. Do I need one of these?
2. What should I look for in one of these if I do need one?

We shall now explore some general criteria that should form the basis of any thinking about the acquisition of equipment.

What the equipment does

It is necessary to establish what an item, such as a copier, can normally be expected to do, as well as what specific models that are under examination as potential purchases do. Functionality is a prime consideration; this is explored further in relation to specific types of equipment.

Generation of the equipment

The technology underlying all equipment develops over years. Today's typewriter, for instance, is very different from the model that is ten years old. As new computer models enter the market-place, leaps are evident in their processing power and storage capacity. An older generation of equipment may possess all the features necessary to meet your needs, and, indeed may be available at very attractive discounts. Last year's models may represent a good buy, but they should only be purchased in full knowledge of the features that have been sacrificed by spurning the latest model.

Compatibility of the equipment

Compatibility may be assessed at both function and design levels. Compatibility at the functional level is clearly an issue with regard to computer equipment, where hardware and software must work together. Desks, chairs and other furniture need to be compatible with one another in both the functional and the design sense. A common design style will enhance the appearance of the office. The preferred height of a chair is influenced by the height of the desk with which it will be used.

Design of the equipment

This has both ergonomic and aesthetic aspects. Ergonomically, it is important that computers have detachable keyboards, photocopiers have feed mechanisms at the correct height and filing cabinets are easy to use. Aesthetically, design influences the general ambience of the office and the image that is conveyed to visitors. Everybody deserves to work, and works better, in a pleasant working environment. Design may have an impact on working practices, efficiency and staff motivation.

Reliability

All equipment will break down or malfunction at some time in its life. A well-chosen piece of equipment will not start to become unreliable until it has given several years' faithful service and is nearing the time when it should be pensioned off. Reliability cannot easily be predicted, but making use of reputable manufacturers and suppliers reduces the risks.

Support

When equipment is not as reliable as was hoped, maintenance and support arrangements can help to overcome problems. Support is most often required during the start-up phase, when the equipment is being installed and its features are still being explored. In relation to computer systems, support may include special training sessions. A telephone help-line, or the opportunity to call out for assistance, particularly during installation, may be available as part of a package or as an optional extra. Support is particularly important if you are new to a given kind of equipment, and your need for support should determine how much it is worth investing in it. If you are a complete novice, always ensure that you have sufficient support to get the most out of your equipment.

Maintenance

Everybody needs some maintenance arrangements to cover essential items of office equipment. The type of arrangement that is appropriate varies with the kind of equipment, how central the equipment is to the activities of the organisation, the portability of the equipment and the predicted reliability of the equipment. Maintenance arrangements can be divided into two types:

1. Maintenance contracts with a variety of call-out arrangements and extents of coverage of labour and parts costs. A contract should guarantee fairly speedy service.
2. Authorised agents who will mend equipment when it goes wrong. The quality and speed of these agents varies, and the service that they offer may be inconveniently slow.

Servicing

Regular servicing of equipment is essential. This may be undertaken as part of a maintenance contract, as part of a special service agreement or by staff using the equipment. Neglect of servicing can shorten the life of the equipment, and, in many cases, will make it less effective or efficient in use.

Reputation

Talk to other people about the equipment they use. If the equipment is old but still reliable, note the manufacturer. Read test reports in business and computer equipment magazines. Use a local library to locate current and recent issues of such magazines if necessary. Perusal of such test reports not only identifies the strengths and weaknesses of the models under review but also develops a checklist of features to seek, and suggests the kind of questions for which answers should be sought from suppliers. The reputation of both manufacturers and suppliers should be considered.

Cost

Normally, you get what you pay for. However, this does not mean that the most expensive is the best, since the best choice depends upon what you want.

Supplies

Expenditure does not stop with the purchase of the equipment. When considering the cost of equipment, the cost of supplies also needs to be taken into account. The difference in paper costs may, for instance, eliminate any margins in the capital outlay associated with two copiers.

Options for the acquisition of office equipment

Where economy is paramount, options for the acquisition of office equipment other than purchase are worth considering. In addition to the purchase of new equipment, the following options are available.

Purchase of second-hand equipment

A number of outlets sell second-hand equipment, but the price and quality can vary significantly. Use a reputable supplier who offers equipment that has been overhauled and serviced. A guarantee should also be sought with some kinds of equipment, such as copiers and typewriters. Second-hand equipment will probably suffer from one or both of the following drawbacks:

1. The image and styling may be old-fashioned.
2. The functions and the underlying technology may be outmoded.

The extent to which these factors present a problem depends on the type of equipment and the significance of its image in a particular office.

Acquisition of second- (or third-) hand equipment free

Sometimes some items of office equipment may be acquired by a small business just setting up from friends or from a larger organisation that might be closing down some of its offices. Clearly, items acquired via this means need to be tested to ensure that they still function properly. Provided equipment is operational, it may be a great boon in the early days of a new business because it is free! Such equipment, while possibly being past its best, may allow the new business time to assess its office equipment needs before committing itself to expenditure. However, in the longer term, free equipment will normally need to be replaced, since it is likely to be old-fashioned in styling and functionality, and may become unreliable.

Leasing new equipment

Many of the larger items of office equipment can be leased from leasing organisations. Leasing arrangements vary, but, typically, an annual leasing fee is fixed and a contract is arranged. The advantages of leasing are:

- Expenditure on office equipment is more evenly distributed over the years.
- Leases can be terminated when the requirement for a given piece of equipment no longer exists.
- As new models become available, the next year's lease can be arranged in respect of the newer models.
- There may be an option to buy the machine cheaply at the expiry of the lease, or to renew the lease at a greatly reduced rate.
- Any tax benefits that might accrue from a leasing arrangement, as compared with capital expenditure.

The potential pitfalls of leasing are:

- You may not own the equipment even after leasing it for a number of years.
- The monthly costs of leasing may be comparable to, or even more than, the cost of the appropriate loan repayments if the item was bought outright with a loan.
- The leasing contract may involve a long-term commitment.
- Leasing may offer inflexible finance arrangements and high interest rates when compared to a bank loan or overdraft.
- Penalty clauses in the event of early settlement where it is decided to change machines prior to the expiry of the original lease may operate.
- Explicit agreements as to when the contract terminates may be absent.

In summary, before embarking on a leasing arrangement, look carefully at the terms of the lease and compare the cost of leasing with the other available options.

Renting

Renting may be a flexible short-term option, although rental contracts tend to cover two or three years. Rental arrangements tend to be the norm for some equipment, such as large copiers.

Most offices will choose to adopt a selection of acquisition options, employing different options for different types of equipment.

A strategy for the selection of office equipment

In addition to the general criteria outlined earlier, the business owner/manager needs a strategy for the selection of office equipment. A five-point strategy is offered here. This simple framework should make explicit the steps in the decision-making process, to facilitate communication with staff and suppliers. A similar but more detailed and focused strategy is also proposed in Chapter 4 for the acquisition of computer-based systems.

If a major system such as a network of computers is being planned, the advice of a consultant may be sought, but on other occasions business owners/managers will have to rely on their own judgement. Even if external advice is available, remember that an outsider does not know your business well enough to make firm recommendations concerning your requirements. Anyone who pretends to do so is merely trying to sell something.

The five-point strategy is:

1. Definition of objectives
2. Exploring the options
3. Narrowing the field
4. Implementation
5. Evaluation.

Definition of objectives

The first stage is the definition of the objectives of the organisation when it is contemplating the acquisition of an item of equipment. Typical general objectives are to get a job done more efficiently or effectively, or to eliminate the need to recruit additional staff. Specific objectives will be concerned with the details of the job to be done. For example, when considering copiers, it might be appropriate to specify the quality of the finished product, the time that it takes to produce one copy or, say, 100 copies, the paper required and the option of colour printing.

Once general objectives have been established, a requirements specification can be developed. This should outline the required and essential features of the item of equipment to be acquired. The specification should be developed co-operatively through dialogue with employees whose job will be affected. The requirements specification may be a checklist of points on one sheet of paper, or a multi-volume document, depending on the scale of the project, but a written specification should always be prepared.

Exploring the options

Armed with a requirements specification, you are in a strong position to tackle the business equipment salesman. You may not be an expert on office equipment, but you should be an expert on what you want to do with it. The objective of this stage is to find out about the models on the market-place, including their prices and features. This process can be time-consuming, so it is important to allocate and control time strictly. Collect sufficient information so that you feel confident that you have reviewed all the major options, and are aware of the best suppliers and models.

Business and computer suppliers should be a good source of information on models and prices. If a convenient exhibition is being mounted, this provides an opportunity to meet suppliers gathered together at one location, which facilitates further contact points and comparisons. A number of periodicals also review business and computer equipment. Other reference sources, such as directories, Yellow Pages, and textbooks, supply other contact points. Occasionally, a seminar may offer the opportunity to observe demonstrations.

At the conclusion of this stage, you should have gathered information about the possibilities and their penalties, in terms of cost, which can be used to refine the requirements specification. You can then prepare to advance to the next stage.

Narrowing the field

This is the time when, in the light of more complete knowledge of the options and the requirements, decisions can be taken. Prior to decisions to purchase, however, it will probably be necessary to:

- draft a short list of the potential models
- examine these models in more detail through demonstrations and additional discussions with suppliers
- work out, with the participation of involved staff, how the equipment will affect current working practices
- work out how to implement the equipment or get it working, again with consultation
- consider maintenance and servicing arrangements.

This stage concludes with the placing of appropriate orders.

Implementation

Shortly after the equipment has been ordered it should arrive! Implementation should have been planned during the third stage; earlier plans can now be put into operation.
Implementation involves:

- any necessary modifications to the environment, such as new wiring, new furniture etc
- installing and testing the equipment
- trial operation of the equipment
- training and introducing staff to the equipment and its objectives, covering both how it works and what it is expected that it will be used for.

It concludes with the equipment 'going live', or going into operation.

Evaluation

Most owners/managers, once an item of equipment is up and running, succumb to the temptation to forget about it until it goes wrong. Unless a large installation of equipment is involved, evaluation need not be an intrusive activity, but it should not be overlooked completely. A log of breakdowns, problems and maintenance activities can provide useful management information, including when an item of equipment should be replaced. A mental note, or a formal schedule, to review the operation of an item of equipment once a year, to assess whether it is still working efficiently and continues to meet the business's objectives, is useful.

Office reprographic systems

Reprographics is the reproduction and handling of all copy documents, at all stages from creation of the copies through to finishing and distribution. Every organisation has a need for some facilities for reproducing copies of documents.

For the small business owner/manager, a crucial decision is which copying should be conducted in-house and which should be placed in the hands of an external agency such as a print shop. Here, the conventional distinction between duplicating and copying can be helpful. Duplicating processes involve the preparation of a master before copies can be made. Copiers work straight from the original. Almost every business needs in-house copying facilities, but some types of duplicating are likely to be placed outside. We shall consider the options for duplicating and copying in turn.

Duplicating

Typical duplicating jobs that might be done outside a small organisation include the printing of letterheads, blank forms, compliment slips, business cards, brochures, price lists and advertising material. If large numbers of copies are required, reports, staff handbooks and telephone lists may also be printed externally.

Duplicating methods are only of passing interest if the business contracts out its duplicating. Nevertheless, it is worth being aware of the options, both to aid communication with print shops and to enable you to decide when and if the transition to in-house duplicating is appropriate.

Methods of duplication can be divided into three groups:

1. *Spirit duplicating* is the simplest and least expensive method, but it is rarely used in business today because it produces a poor quality copy. The process uses a plain paper master. The plain paper is placed on hectographic carbon paper, carbon side uppermost, and the material to be duplicated is written, drawn or typed on to the plain paper. A carbon image is thus created on the reverse of the paper. The master is placed in the duplicator where the spirit dissolves small amounts of the carbon deposit on to the copy.

2. *Stencil duplicating* works on the principle of ink passing through finely cut images on a very thin sheet of cellulose paper lightly coated with a special wax. Stencils are cut with a typewriter, by typing on to them, by heat transfer or by electronic means. Lengthier runs are possible with stencil duplication than with spirit duplication, although, again, the quality of the output is more suited to internal than external use.

3. *Offset duplicating* or lithography provides a professional finish and is therefore the most appropriate method for most jobs. The master is attached to a large roller and then inked up; the image is offset on to a second roller. This second roller comes into contact with a third roller which feeds through blank paper, on to which the copy is deposited. The process depends critically on the correct mix of ink and acid/water solution which separates the non-image area on the plate. Operator skill in inking the rollers and adjusting the flow of fluid is essential. Offset duplicating also involves making plates. Paper plates can be prepared by hand or on the typewriter, but the most common method is by electrostatic photocopier. Paper plates are easy to produce and are suitable for many applications. Where exceptionally long runs are required, metal plates can be made via chemical or diffusion transfer. Lithography produces high quality copies and will

cater for print runs of several thousand copies. Machines may be manual, semi-automatic or completely automatic, and table-top models are available.

Copying

There is an extensive range of copying equipment on the market. Copiers can be grouped into three categories:

1. Small, simple desk-top models for the small user (under 1000 copies per month)
2. Low, mid and high volume copiers (1000 to 30,000 copies per month)
3. Giant copiers (over 100,000 copies per month).

The volume of copying required is of central concern in the selection of copying equipment. Other factors to be considered are listed in Checklist 3.1.

Most copies operate with plain paper. The few electrostatic copiers still on the market, which take special sensitised paper, may be a tempting buy, but their running costs are such that they are unlikely to be a good investment, unless usage is very low volume.

All businesses should have a service contract on copiers. Be wary about signing service contracts that commit you to the same dealer for a long period. Prices for service contracts vary, so it is worth shopping around. The contracts for both the rental agreement and the service agreement should be signed at the same time, to ensure that all clauses are satisfactory.

Photocopying machines are prone to misuse if they are available for general use in an office. Likely problems and possible solutions are summarised in Table 3.1.

Checklist 3.1 *Features to examine in copiers*

1. Speed with which copies are produced.
2. Maximum paper size taken.
3. Paper-feed arrangement.
4. Reduction and enlargement facilities.

5. Bypass facility to feed through single sheets.
6. Ability to copy on both sides of the paper (known as duplexing).
7. Potential to copy in colour. Machines are available which will make full-colour copies, but they are expensive.
8. Automatic document feed, where the copier will select and position the original on the glass, eject it when completed and continue with the next original.
9. Automatic selection, where the copier will automatically match the original to the appropriate paper size.
10. Job recovery, or the ability to restart automatically without the need to reset the number required after a paper jam.
11. Quality of the product in terms of contrast, cleanness of the paper and distinctness of characters. Ideally, the copy should be indistinguishable from or even better than the original.

Table 3.1 *Misuse of photocopiers – some common problems*

Problem	Solution
Failure to operate the machine correctly, leading to breakdown	Better training of users
Unnecessary copying	Improve filing system and communication
Excessive copying, or running off extra copies 'just in case'	Easy access to machine for additional copies
Uneconomic use of the machine, eg failure to reduce size	Inform staff of actual copying costs
Private or unauthorised use of the machine	Implement a copy control or monitoring system.

Support equipment for copying and duplicating

There are a number of items of support equipment which facilitate the paper handling associated with copying and duplicating. These include:

1. *Collating machines*, for arranging multiple-page documents in order.
2. *Joggers*, for accurately aligning sets of papers prior to stapling or binding.
3. *Binding machines*. Three common kinds are available: the spiral binder, the flat-comb binder and the thermal effect perfect binder, where papers are bound by an adhesive seal extending along the spine of the cover.
4. *Lettering machines*, which prepare adhesive strips of letters to be attached to the page.
5. *Laminating machines*, which coat pages with a protective clear plastic seal. These are used to seal a cover to make it more durable.

Typewriters

The typewriter has in recent years been largely superseded by word processors. Word processors are more flexible than typewriters, permitting much easier editing and correction. Nevertheless, typewriters have some value in offices for completing pre-printed forms and creating short letters, memos and invoices. Another advantage of the typewriter over the word processor is the significant price differential.

When considering the purchase of a typewriter, the following characteristics of the modern machine should be taken into account:

1. *The introduction of single-element machines*, where the carriage remains stationary and the single element (such as a daisy wheel) moves backwards and forwards along a bar inside the machine, thereby producing the print. Golf balls and daisy-wheels can be changed easily, so that it is possible to introduce different typefaces and sizes. The

character spacing and the availability of proportional spacing can also be easily changed.

2. *The introduction of correcting features.* Backspacing moves the element to the error and a lift-off correcting ribbon can be activated to lift the error from the page.

3. *Keyboard improvements.* Although the traditional QWERTY arrangement has persisted, much effort has been directed towards the design of keyboards, with a view to maximising user comfort. The size and shape of keys, their distance apart and the slope of the keyboard may all contribute to ease of use.

4. *Size and weight.* A lighter, compact typewriter is often more appropriate if the typewriter is being used alongside word-processing facilities.

Typewriters can be divided into four categories:

1. *Portable typewriters*, which may be either manual or electric, can be stored in a case and moved from one place to another. Portable typewriters are often the cheapest option, but may not offer as wide a range of features as other models. Provided they are sufficiently robust and stable, they can be a useful adjunct to other text-processing facilities, or may be suitable as a home machine.

2. *Electric typewriters* are the mainstay standard office typewriter, but they are gradually being replaced by electronic typewriters, memory typewriters and word processors.

3. *Electronic typewriters.* An electronic typewriter is a cross between an electric typewriter and a word processor. It looks like an electric typewriter, but incorporates a microprocessor which gives it a basic memory. This memory may be a correction-only memory designed to make lift-off correction as described earlier, or it may be able to store frequently occurring phrases and short paragraphs and offer editing facilities.

4. *Memory typewriters* are intermediate between typewriters and word processors. Such typewriters have a memory and single-line displays showing about 30 characters.

The larger the memory, the closer the facilities are likely to be to those of a word processor. The most appropriate machines are those with a memory of approximately 8000 characters. If more memory is required, a word processor is probably the best solution.

Many electronic and memory typewriters can be upgraded to word processors by adding disk drives and a visual display unit, but it is cheaper to purchase a word processor or microcomputer with word-processing software.

Checklist 3.2 *Some standard features of electronic typewriters*

1. Different carriage lengths are available.
2. Single-line display, so that a line can be displayed and edited before it is committed to paper.
3. Automatic centring.
4. Decimal tabulation, so that figures can be lined up at the decimal point.
5. Automatic underscore, where characters can be selected for underlining automatically as they are typed.
6. Half-spacing.
7. Justified right-hand margin, so that the margin is straight.
8. Emboldening, where words may be emphasised by the wheel striking the ribbon twice for each letter.
9. Automatic paper insertion and alignment, so that the text on each page can start at the same position.
10. Repeater keys, so that the same character can be repeated by continuing to press the key.
11. Automatic carriage return.
12. Stop code, so that the printing of a paragraph called from memory can be halted in order to make modifications, and later, the printing resumed.
13. Automatic column calculation, where the position of the tab stops is automatically calculated on the basis of the largest phrase in each column.

Word processors

The main functions of word processors are the creation, storage, retrieval and subsequent editing of text. A word processor then supports the creation and subsequent rearrangement, revision, correction and updating of text. This includes:

- merging of lists of names and addresses with standard letters to produce personalised documents
- maintaining and updating databases of information, sorting and rearranging the data
- building documents from stored blocks of text.

There are two main types of word-processing configuration: dedicated word processors and microcomputers running word-processing software. Both options incorporate memory, keyboards, VDUs and printers. Typically, dedicated word processors have special keyboards with a range of special function keys which are labelled with the action to be performed, such as 'COPY', 'FILE' and 'DELETE'; the keyboard layout needs to support extensive text inputting. On a microcomputer, function keys are labelled with codes, such as 'PF1', 'PF2', and the user needs to memorise the function of these keys. Some dedicated word-processing systems offer a full A4 screen, which can be very attractive for viewing complete pages of documents.

Dedicated word processors were a sensible choice when the word-processing software on microcomputers was less user-friendly than it is today. For most small businesses, however, a microcomputer is the most flexible and economic purchase, and facilitates the creation of documents comprising a mixture of spreadsheets, graphics, data and text.

Word processing is further developed in the context of word-processing software in Chapter 4 on the electronic office. Components of word-processing systems, such as keyboards, VDUs, memory and printers, are discussed in more detail in the same chapter.

Dictation/transcription equipment

Dictation and transcription equipment is primarily intended for use with audio-typing. A dictating machine records speech for subsequent playback by a typist who can listen to the material and simultaneously type what is heard.

Since a dictating machine is a means of recording the human voice, it may have other uses. It might be used for leaving messages, in rehearsing speeches, for brainstorming original ideas, to make sales reports, to make verbal notes on-site such as in stocktaking or surveying, and as a means of recording important or complicated telephone conversations.

There are three main types of dictating machine: portable, desk-top and centralised. Portable and desk-top models are the most suitable for the small business. The portable dictation unit costs less and is convenient. Desk-top models are usually more sturdy and reliable, and offer more features. Playback can be through a loudspeaker or through a microphone in conjunction with a foot control and headset. Fast forward and fast rewind buttons, voice, pitch and speed control level buttons are all helpful. Centralised equipment is used in larger organisations with a typing pool.

Most dictating equipment uses magnetic media for storage, so that disks and tapes can be edited and reused. Microcassettes may store 15, 30 or 60 minutes on each side, and some dictation units operate on standard cassettes. The equipment and the cassettes must be compatible with one another.

Indexing of audio cassettes is necessary; the typist must be able to locate specific positions in the document. The position of documents may be marked on the cassette, or a counter or display may assist in locating documents.

Dictating equipment should economise on both the dictators' and the typists' time. The dictator can record documents whenever it is convenient. However, one of the main disadvantages of dictation equipment is that it tends to eliminate person-to-person contact, which is important in a successful working relationship. Other problems may arise if the typist and the dictator have not been adequately trained in the use of the equipment.

When selecting dictating equipment, it is important to establish who will use it and how it will be used. Compatibility with other audio equipment should be maintained. The fidelity of the recordings and typical lengths of recordings are other factors to consider, and finally, back-up and service support from the supplier is desirable.

Calculators

Major calculations will probably be performed with the aid of a computer, or electronic calculating machine, but calculators remain useful for small-scale calculating and checking.

Calculators are available in many shapes and sizes to suit every pocket. All calculators can add, subtract, multiply, divide and work out percentages. Some also have a programmable memory to store formulae for complex calculations. Special functions, such as statistical functions or general scientific or mathematical functions, are also available on some calculators. Pocket calculators display answers on a liquid crystal display. Some desk-top calculators also print results on a tally roll. This can be useful in checking and error detection.

The keyboard or keypad must be large enough for keys to be depressed individually. Special features might include a raised dot on the centre key to aid touch operation and a function key for selecting the number of decimal places.

Most calculators are battery operated and most have an automatic cut-off facility. Some desk-top varieties may also be run off the mains.

Mailing equipment

Equipment needed to handle incoming mail is relatively modest. Even in a large organisation, this is not likely to extend to more than a letter-opening machine, stapling machines, date stamps, sorting trays and delivery trolleys. This may be supplemented by copying machines for taking copies and a shredder for shredding envelopes for recycling.

Outgoing mail might require some of the following items:

- letter scales
- parcel scales
- collating machines
- joggers

- folding machines to fold publicity material etc
- addressing machines to produce addresses for labels during large mailings.
- seal machines to seal envelopes
- inserting machines
- parcel-tying (banding) machines
- franking machines, to produce a postage stamp imprint of an appropriate denomination.

Rubber stamps

Rubber stamps are cheap and can save a lot of time. It is worth investing in rubber stamps for:

- addresses of major customers
- your own name and address, to stamp on the back of envelopes for various other occasions (this operation can also be performed by a slub inserted in your franking machine)
- date stamp
- numbering devices
- Freepost
- First Class Post.

A stamp tidy is also useful.

Supplies

Supplies include a wide range of consumables, such as paper, staples, pens, Blutak, drawing pins and computer paper. Some of these need to be reordered more frequently than others. Sufficient stocks need to be kept so that you never run out of crucial items but, on the other hand, excessive stocks of supplies should be avoided. They may spoil, or become redundant as the equipment with which they are used is replaced.

To help preserve appropriate stocks of supplies, it is a good idea to keep a record of current stocks and previous orders. A stock card may be maintained for each item. This card can give the maximum and minimum figures for ordering. The maximum is the maximum order to be placed at any one time, while the minimum is the stock level at which more supplies should be ordered.

It is important to locate a good supplier who can meet all your needs. Look for good quality at a competitive price. Once you have found a satisfactory supplier, you are unlikely to want to change the supplier, so the initial choice may influence buying over a long period.

Summary

This chapter has outlined some principles to be adopted in the acquisition of office equipment and supplies. Criteria for the selection of some items of equipment are developed in this chapter, but other items are explored more fully in the next two chapters in the context of the electronic office and office communication systems.

4

The Electronic Office

The paperless office

The electronic office, or in its more extreme form, the paperless office, is the focus of many scenarios for the office of the next century. The vision is one of computers, word processors, fax and other terminals linked to each other and a central computer. Office staff will have workstations that communicate with the workstations of other employees, customers, suppliers and banks through internal, national and international telecommunications networks. The technology to establish the paperless office already exists, and offices are making great use of electronic documents, but attempts to establish a paperless office today will be undermined by the following factors:

1. Paper documents coming into the organisation from outside, such as invoices, orders, letters, contracts, leaflets, newsletters and reports.
2. The need to store certain paper documents for security or confidentiality, or legal requirements (the tax inspector has yet to go paperless).
3. The need to output paper documents to other people. Even facsimile transmission machines are just fancy means of transmitting paper documents.
4. People prefer paper for some kinds of reading and reference. It is portable and easier to read in various environments, such as on the train, in the armchair or at meetings. It is easier to annotate and compare two documents. Significant efforts have been put into making access to electronic documents as convenient as paper, but paper still has its attractions.

Today's office is an amalgam of the electronic office and the more traditional paper-based office.

Computers can reduce the amount of paper used in information processing in an office, speed the production of documents and facilitate better access to the information contained in the documents, but will not eliminate paper.

This chapter first explores when a computer might be useful and then considers what characteristics to look for in hardware and software.

When do you need a computer?

The heart of the electronic office is the computer. Later in this chapter some of the types of computer system that might be appropriate for an office in a small organisation will be reviewed. The first step is to consider the reasons for acquiring a computer system. These will normally be a combination of:

- a need to process information and documents more quickly and efficiently
- a need to produce additional documents, improve access to information or generally adopt an alternative method of information processing.

The acquisition of a computer system is often triggered by the appeal of a word processor. As compared with a typewriter, a word processor supports easier correction and creation of documents, and thus more flexible production of letters, reports and publicity material. The other applications of computers are multifarious: databases and spreadsheets are particularly worth considering. Most businesses can benefit from a small database of contacts containing names and addresses, telephone numbers, interests and other business details. Other databases might cover stock held, work completed and staff details. Spreadsheets are essentially electronic tables which can be used to handle and manipulate numerical and statistical data. Once the small business owner/manager has uncovered the delights of word processing, databases and spreadsheets, other applications such as electronic diaries, electronic mail, desk-top publishing and graphics can be explored.

Setting up a new computer system always takes time. At the outset, a significant learning effort will be required. This is time-consuming, and the time can be profitably spent elsewhere unless the benefits of computerisation are clearly evident. The average business owner/manager does not need to know anything about electronics or programming, but he must grasp the basics of the software that will be used, know how to check that the computer is correctly installed, that all components of the system are compatible with one another, and, often, the most troublesome element of all, know how to keep the printer working!

There are two hazards that need to be negotiated. The first is the amount of money that can be absorbed in the acquisition of this refinement and that add-on. When examining a starter system, look at the complete price for the system that will do what you want it to, and not just the price of the computer or word processor. The second problem is the amount of time that can be wasted in the initial phase of the life of a system, especially if things do not work as they should.

Small businesses should start to consider computers when large numbers of contracts, supplies or transactions need to be recorded. Typically, such businesses may have:

- many customers or suppliers
- many orders
- many quotations, which are compiled from standard components
- large numbers of items in stock and frequent reordering
- much or frequent financial analysis
- large numbers of calculations
- many agents or employees
- complicated records
- much drafting and revision of documents
- a need to present numerical information in the form of charts
- many personalised letters, quotations and other documents.

Computers may also be used in some trades and professions for specialised functions such as computer-aided design. If your business does not display any of the above characteristics, then computerisation is probably inappropriate. Instead, spend some time devising appropriate card indexes. Card indexes, calculators and portable typewriters, while lacking a high-tech image, are useful tools for creating short documents, keeping simple records and doing a limited number of calculations.

Computer systems

All computer systems comprise:

- hardware, or the basic equipment which makes up the system
- software, or the instructions or programs that tell the computer what to do.

First, we shall focus our attention on hardware, leaving software until later. All computer systems can be represented by the simple model in Figure 4.1, in which the system can be seen to have four essential components:

1. *Input devices*, such as keyboards, light pens, mice, graphics tablets, and optical and image character recognition devices. Input devices convert data intelligible to humans into a form that can be handled by the computer.
2. *Central processing unit*, or CPU, which, in turn, comprises:
   - the control unit, which exercises overall control over the operation of the system
   - the arithmetic or logic unit, which performs arithmetic operations and logical comparisons on the data held in the main memory
   - the main memory or immediate access store, which holds the information currently being processed and the programs needed for the processing.
3. *Auxiliary or external storage*, such as hard and floppy disks, which is used to store the data once processing is complete, so that the data can be recalled at a later date.
4. *Output devices*, such as printers and visual display units

(VDUs), which output data in a form that is appropriate for people to use. Floppy disks and other magnetic storage media can also be regarded as input and output media, since data can be output from one system, on to, say, a floppy disk, and then input into another system by placing that disk in another computer.

Figure 4.1 *The basic computer configuration*

Auxiliary or external storage

$\updownarrow$

Input devices $\leftrightarrow$ Central processing unit $\leftrightarrow$ Output devices

Computers are divided into three categories on the basis of their processing power: mainframes, minicomputers and microcomputers. Microcomputers are likely to be of most interest to the small business. Larger mainframes and minicomputers are more appropriate in a larger organisation where systems have many users and are used for a wide variety of different kinds of application.

Microcomputers may be run as stand-alone machines, where the computer operates independently of any other machine, or as part of a network. Once a small business has outgrown one microcomputer, the desirability of a network should be assessed. Two or three unlinked machines may be adequate, thus avoiding the need to tangle with networks. In many applications, however, a network can be useful to allow more than one workstation to share resources. Typically, a network supports access to a shared database, shared hard-disk storage, networked software or a shared printer. The cost of a network can be offset against savings from the purchase of fewer printers, or savings on the purchase of multiple copies of software. The installation of networks is a specialist topic and expert advice should be sought. Some further discussion of local area networks is included in Chapter 5 which deals with communication.

What to look for in a computer

To return to the basic microcomputer, what criteria need to be applied in its selection? The most important criteria in selection appertain to your specific application; you need to think in terms of the requirements of your application, before investigating the market-place. Nevertheless, there are some general criteria that are worth outlining.

The watchword is compatibility. At the very least, the hardware must be compatible with the software that will be run on it. If this software is one of the standard business software packages, then a 100 per cent IBM PC compatible machine is a sensible and flexible purchase. Certain desk-top publishing software packages are specifically designed for the Apple Macintosh and its equivalents, although IBM PC compatible versions are usually also available. Some software will run on a range of other machines, so familiarity with a particular type of machine may mean that that machine is a sensible acquisition.

Apart from compatibility, other main considerations are reliability, price, and dealer back-up and support. A maintenance contract at around 10 per cent of the purchase price is also highly advisable, especially if the business has only one machine which is in relatively heavy demand. The maintenance contract should offer fairly fast response and on-site repair. When selecting a maintenance contract, remember to pay for what you want, bearing in mind that a computer out of action for a week may be a catastrophe at a particularly busy time, if you have all your business data stored on that computer and are relying on it to produce invoices and other standard documents.

Compatibility, reliability, price, maintenance and support are always valuable. The other characteristics that might be sought are less immutable. Models available in the market-place change regularly. You can guarantee that if you wait another six months you will be able to purchase a better machine at a much lower cost. But, if you can afford to wait six months, then you probably do not need a computer anyway! It is important to acquire a computer that meets your present requirements, and is likely to be compatible with future models, so that databases can be transferred from one model to the next as necessary. End-of-the-line models may be available at significant discounts. These may be a good buy, provided that they are appropriate for the application and compatible with later technology.

Some general guidelines to be considered when examining computer hardware are:

1. *Storage capacity*. Buy a hard-disk machine, with as large a hard disk as you can afford. Storage capacity is measured in kilobytes (thousands of bytes) and megabytes (millions of bytes). One byte of storage holds approximately one character of text. When calculating storage requirements, it is necessary to consider the space occupied by software, as well as any other storage overheads associated with the application, such as index files for databases. Hard disks are typically 20, 40 or 80 megabytes. A 40-megabyte hard disk should be sufficient for many basic business applications. Databases tend to consume a lot of storage space, so allow more storage space for database applications. It is possible to expand the hard disk storage capacity later, but it is more satisfactory and usually cheaper to start with the appropriate capacity.

2. *Processing power*, or the capacity of the random access memory (RAM). This will determine what can be done with the machine. Software packages have minimum configurations on which they can be run.

3. *Ease of use of keyboard*. Look at:
   - the size of the keys
   - the separation between the keys
   - the key travel
   - the availability of function keys and separate numeric keypads
   - the flexibility in, and the angle of, the keyboard.

4. *Monitors* (or VDUs). Great advances have been made in monitors in recent years. Monochrome monitors are available with amber, green or white displays. It is worth paying for a high-resolution monochrome display. The trend is towards colour monitors with high-resolution

graphics facilities. Naturally, the better the resolution of the image on the monitor, the higher the price. You must decide how much you are prepared to pay. Opinion is divided concerning the desirability of colour monitors in everyday use. At the barest minimum, it should be possible to distinguish between similar characters such as I and 1, 2 and Z, and O and Q. Brightness must be controllable and the image must be stable (ie not flicker).

Again, it is important that the software package that you intend to run is displayed effectively on a given monitor. Some software that is designed for colour monitors with good graphics facilities does not work well with more basic monitors.

5. *Operating system under which the system runs.* UNIX, MS-DOS and PC-DOS are well-known operating systems for microcomputers. The operating system determines the basic facilities offered by the computer and the software that can be run on the computer, since any software must be compatible with the operating system.

6. *Type of printer.* Printers are a law unto themselves. Printers are important, since print-outs may be despatched far and wide, and therefore may influence the image that the business projects. There are three kinds of printer that are likely to be considered by the small business: daisy wheel, dot matrix and laser.

Daisy-wheel printers have a print quality similar to good quality conventional typewriters, but they are slow. Twenty characters per second is typical; that amounts to about one minute per A4 page. As the print quality of dot-matrix printers has improved, daisy-wheel printers are being outpaced.

Dot-matrix printers print letters as a series of dots. Typically, dot-matrix printers offer a range of settings with different print quality at different speeds. For example, draft quality (ie rather rough) may be available at 160 characters per second and near letter quality (NLQ) at 25 to 30 characters per second. A printer must at least be capable of producing NLQ. The quality of NLQ varies from one printer to another, so the output from a printer should be examined, preferably in a working environment, rather than in the showroom or at an exhibition.

Laser printers are within the reach of the larger business. The print quality is very good, with a wide range of type founts and sizes. Many laser printers are still rather slow, though, and a laser printer is likely to be used in conjunction with another printer. The laser printer can be called upon for high quality print jobs, while a dot-matrix printer might be used for the more routine work.

Clearly, quality and speed are two central issues in the selection of a printer. The faster the better, but you have to pay for speed. If draft quality is acceptable for most documents, then a dot-matrix printer that produces reasonable draft quality at a good speed may be appropriate. However, before committing yourself to a cheap printer, think carefully about how much time will be wasted in printing a 50-page document, and then decide whether this can be tolerated. Quality can be judged by the clarity of the print and the range of typefaces and type sizes.

7. *Other input devices.* These are used to supplement the keyboard; they are not meant to act as a substitute. A mouse is useful with software that is designed to work with a mouse. A mouse is a small box with buttons on the top. By moving the mouse around the desk top, the cursor can be controlled on the display screen. To select an operation or an option from a menu, the cursor is pointed at the selection and by pressing one of the buttons the selection is automatically activated. A mouse is easy to use, but may interrupt work-flow since one hand has to be taken off the keyboard. A mouse is not usually essential.

Data can also be input by magnetic character recognition, light pens used with bar codes and touch-sensitive screens. These have specialist applications. One area to watch, however, is optical character recognition, where there have recently been significant advances in technology. Optical character recognition (OCR) allows documents to be read straight into the computer store, thereby eliminating a lot of keying in of data. Equipment is still expensive, but the future looks promising.

8. *Space factors and environmental considerations* need to be taken into account. Additional desk space is likely to be necessary, and the introduction of a computer system will probably cause modifications to the layout and work flow of the office. Different systems will have differing effects.

9. *Ease of operation* is clearly important, especially to the new computer user.

10. *Ease of installation* may be difficult to assess, but nevertheless needs to be considered.

11. *Cost*, both initial outlay and ongoing costs, needs to be considered.

12. *Potential for enhancement* is closely related to compatibility, and should be discussed at an early stage. As your business grows, the computing needs of the business will also evolve.

Portable microcomputers and others

Portable microcomputers have been on the market for several years. Two categories of portable machine are available: laptops and notepads, laptops being the larger of the two. Portable means 'can be moved from one location to another'. As with a portable television, while it may be possible to move the computer, it may not do you any good! If portability is important, consider the weight and size of the machine carefully. Portability may be desirable when different people need to use a machine and want to move it from one office to another, or when one person wishes to use the machine in different locations, such as in the office, at home or on the train. Also, since portables are small, they are compact and do not occupy as much desk space as a desk-top machine.

Portables can be used as a machine in their own right or as a data-entry unit for recording data on floppy disks. In the latter case, the data might subsequently be read, stored and printed with the intervention of a desk-top machine. Portables are more expensive for equivalent processing power than a desk-top machine and on the cheaper models, screen quality has to be sacrificed. Portable microcomputers should only be considered when portability is a priority.

There is also a variety of other small processors in the market-place. Time managers, calendars, translators, dictionaries and diaries may be worth considering if you have a particular need for this kind of tool.

Software and what it should do

Software is the instructions to the computer which tell it how to operate and what to do. Software comes in two categories: systems software and applications software. Systems software or the operating system (OS) is the set of programs that is stored in the computer's internal memory; it controls the basic operation of the computer. Loading the operating system has been described as breathing life into the computer.

Applications software is software written to support a particular kind of application, such as word processing or database creation. A computer system needs both systems software and applications software, and the two must be compatible with one another.

The operating system allows access to programs and data which are kept as files both in the computer memory and on disks. Each file has a name and files may be grouped into directories. A directory is the equivalent of a folder in a filing cabinet, while a file is the parallel of a new letter or document. The operating system offers a range of facilities, central to which are:

- creating new directories
- deleting old directories
- creating files
- deleting files
- copying files
- renaming files.

Applications software can be specifically written for a particular organisation, but most software for office applications is available as packages which can be purchased from software suppliers. There are now well-established packages to support most business applications. Experience in using such packages is transferable from one work environment to another, and it should be relatively easy to find staff who are conversant with the well-known packages. A well-established package is usually (but not always) well supported by the software supplier, tried and tested, and accompanied by good documentation. The standard business packages usually offer a good range of features, the only disadvantage being that it may take some time to become familiar with all aspects of the package.

All software is written in a programming language such as FORTRAN, BASIC, 'C', PASCAL, or machine code or assembler. The average computer user does not need to know anything about programming languages. Some database packages incorporate fourth-generation programming languages so that users can design their own applications. Simple applications should be within the scope of the average user, provided that the user wishes to devote the time to developing the application.

Software is central to the system and its selection is crucial. Software has a direct influence on working practices and what can be achieved with the computer system. Software that is difficult to learn, or requires a lot of fiddling around to achieve the desired results, can waste time that is worth more than it cost.

What to look for in software

A number of the criteria that might be applied in the selection of hardware can be reworked in the context of software selection. Again, support is invaluable; price, compatibility and ease of use must all be considered. More specifically, the following should be taken into account:

1. *Support*. To the new software user, support is especially crucial, but even the experienced user will benefit from good documentation and other support materials. Documentation in the form of user manuals should be available with all packages; it should explain all the features of

the package and be easy to follow. Manuals should include a guided tour to the package to assist new users, and a reference section to aid more experienced users in dealing with specific problems. On-screen tutorials and help systems are a welcome extra. With some packages, a maintenance contract, which costs around 10 to 15 per cent of the purchase price, will offer access to additional support. This may take the form of cheap or free upgraded versions of the software, training and help desks. About all else, a software package should be selected that is supported by a supplier who will still be a leader in the market-place in a few years' time, when you might wish to upgrade your application.

2. *Previous experience.* Learning a new software package is time-consuming. Previous experience may be a determining factor in the choice of a package.

3. *Functions of the application.* The features available in the software package must be matched against the requirements of the individual application. This issue will be developed further on page 89 when we consider the specific types of applications software package.

4. *Price.* Most microcomputer packages for business use can be acquired at a relatively modest price. Pricing strategies vary, so it is important to ascertain precisely what the price includes – manuals may be extra. Arrangements for making additional copies need to be heeded. Network software is usually priced in accordance with the number of users or number of workstations on the network.

5. *Compatibility* is sufficiently important to merit a further mention.

6. *Ease of use* of software minimises the time spent in learning and using the package. Good dialogue design, and appropriate use of menus, windows, icons and mice make it easier for the new user to become acclimatised to the package.

Most well-established software packages have been reviewed in the business equipment or personal computing press. Some suppliers make evaluation packages available at a nominal charge, which can be offset against the cost of the full package, when and if it is purchased. In the last analysis, with many business packages it may be worth purchasing two packages and evaluating them both. The cost of two packages is not prohibitive, although indecision may cost dearly in time for learning and evaluation.

Types of applications software package

A number of standard office applications for computers are available. These are demonstrated by the software that is available to support office applications. Software exists to support word processing, database management, spreadsheets, graphics, desk-top publishing, communications, integrated applications, various special-purpose applications and a miscellany of other functions. The various categories of software will be considered in turn.

Word processing

Word processors and word-processing software support the creation, storage, and later recall and modification of text. Typical uses include producing letters – especially standard letters – reports, forms, lists and manuals. Word-processing packages support the manipulation of text, including, for example, alignment of margins, the deletion and insertion of sentences, lines, words and paragraphs, back-up files, underlining and arrange for the text to be appropriately placed on the page. Most software also provides facilities for merging files, arranging records in a file in order according to some criterion and searching for specific strings within small files. More sophisticated word processors will also have: more advanced database-creation facilities: a mailmerge facility for the creation of personalised documents by merging a file of names and addresses with a standard letter; a spell checker or dictionary of words which can be used to locate spelling errors; and, even, a grammar checker which locates grammatical errors. Not all systems show on screen the final version as it will appear when it is printed out, with, for example, emboldening, underlining and right-hand margin justification. 'What You See Is What You Get' (WYSIWYG) means that what's on screen is an exact image of what will be printed. WYSIWYG makes a major contribution to easier document design and is a desirable feature.

Databases

Database software supports the creation of databases and files. Typically, the software holds data in the form of records, which are comprised of fields. For example, a database package may be employed to store details of customers. One record would be created for each customer, and each record might contain a number of fields in which can be stored data such as name, address, telephone number, date of last contact and other notes. Where only a small amount of data needs to be held in a database, a computer is not necessary – remember the simplicity of the card index.

A database package does offer flexibility in retrieval, so that records may, for instance, be selected by location, date of last contact or size of last contract, as well as by name. Also, data may be displayed or printed out in various different formats and in different orders, as required. The order of fields within records, and the order of records themselves, may be changed, from say, customer name order, to order by value of purchases in the previous year, and then changed back again. Reports containing various subsets of the data may be generated.

The cheaper microcomputer-based database packages are described as flat-file systems in that they merely handle databases as separate entities. A database management system (DBMS) has the additional potential to relate two or more databases to one another, so that it is possible, for example, to examine data from more than one database simultaneously, or to use that data, in say, printing an invoice. A DBMS would, for example, support the establishment of two related databases, one containing details of suppliers and another containing the full specification of supplies that might be required. By using data from both databases simultaneously, details of supplies available, such as name, colour and size, may be used together with the name and address of potential suppliers. This relational database facility is a valuable feature for the serious business user.

Time is needed to learn the software and to input data. Setting up a database is time-consuming, but the benefits can be considerable.

Spreadsheets

Spreadsheet packages support the storage and manipulation of numerical data. Spreadsheets are invaluable as a management decision-making tool. They are suitable for storing financial and production data, and can be used to assess the existing situation and to plan for the future.

A spreadsheet is a large table which contains a number of cells arranged in rows and columns. The spreadsheet extends beyond the limits of the screen and can be scrolled horizontally and vertically to examine other parts of the spreadsheet. Numbers, formulae or text such as labels can be entered into the spreadsheet cells. The software allows the user to rearrange data in the rows and columns, and to transfer data between spreadsheets, but most significantly formulae can be entered to perform various arithmetical operations, such as adding columns together or creating another column which shows the effect of a 10 per cent increase on a previous column. Such a facility allows 'What if' questions to be investigated. For example, the user can ask the software to project profits based on a 5 per cent increase in sales, and a percentage decrease in costs, or a change in the rate of VAT, and then perform the same calculations again inserting different percentages. Some spreadsheet packages also offer facilities for graphical presentation, as discussed below with regards to graphics packages.

Graphics software

Graphics software supports the creation of graphs, histograms, pie charts and other graphical analyses of data. When it is desirable to print out the graphics shown on the screen, a dot-matrix printer or, for better results, a graphics plotter may be used. Computer graphics aid the analysis and presentation of data, and may enhance communication with colleagues and clients.

In addition to basic business graphics, there is also a wide range of packages designed for computer-aided design (CAD), which are used by engineers and architects to develop designs.

Desk-top publishing packages

Desk-top publishing (DTP) packages are a popular new entrant to the business software market. They are useful in the preparation of in-house magazines, advertising material, brochures, pamphlets and overhead projector slides. Desk-top publishing software allows the user to create documents, including text and graphics, or to import such documents from word-processing or graphics packages. The desk-top publisher enables the user to design the page for a document in terms of layout, use of vertical and horizontal lines, columns, different type sizes and founts, and art work. Thus, a user can set up a page ready for the printer or for in-house printing. Some desk-top publishing packages store libraries of images for future use, so that logos and other illustrations can be used across a number of documents to establish a house style.

Desk-top publishing is best viewed as a cheaper means of producing small runs of an in-house document, or as a means of setting up a master for external printing. Be warned, however, desk-top publishing is a time-consuming activity, and the time that it absorbs needs to be carefully monitored. Considerable design skills need to be exhibited in the creation of a desk-top published document. You should not be tempted to use all the typefaces on offer in one document! Examine some conventionally printed brochures before embarking on a document design.

Communications software

Communications software is essential if you want to 'talk' to other computers. A number of options are available.

Internal electronic mail software is useful in an organisation where there are several networked computers. Using electronic mail, messages can be transmitted to other network users. Messages are stored until the recipient is ready to read his mail, which will then be displayed on his screen. Internal electronic mail can eliminate much internal paperwork, but is likely to be of limited interest to the very small business.

Other communications software can assist in accessing external computers, such as computers holding large publicly available databases of financial, business or technical information. Only where a small business has a regular requirement for access to such databases will communications software be required.

Integrated software

An integrated software package typically incorporates word-processing, database, spreadsheet, graphics and sometimes communications software as a single package. The chief attraction of an integrated package is the ease with which documents containing a mixture of text, tables and graphics can be created. Also, since only one package needs to be acquired to cover the multitude of business applications, the price may be competitive, and the integrated interface reduces the time spent in learning how to use the package. The problem with integrated packages lies in the quality of their component modules. Often, the word-processing facilities in such packages are good, but the database facilities may be relatively rudimentary and only suitable for building small databases. Also, integrated packages make relatively high demands on storage capacity and processing power. Some of the value of integration has been eroded in recent years, as packages have become more compatible with one another.

Special-purpose software

In addition to the range of standard business software which finds wide application in many offices, some offices may need special-purpose software that has been designed to meet the needs of their particular business. A large proportion of special-purpose software is tailored database software, such as might be employed in an estate agent or a library. Directories of such software are available. Further information on special software can often be obtained from professional or trade associations, or specialist software suppliers.

Other software

Software suppliers are always seeking additonal market niches, and various other software products are available. A number of these are executive toys; others are useful, but a pen and paper would do the job just as well. You may encounter personal information managers, essentially electronic personal organisers, and time information managers, sophisticated diaries.

A strategy for the selection and evaluation of computer systems

A computer system may have a significant influence on the efficiency and effectiveness of the office. The following strategy for the selection and evaluation of computer equipment closely mirrors the strategy outlined in Chapter 3 for all types of office equipment. The same steps as were recommended in Chapter 3 are followed and advice offered there is not reiterated but some areas that need special attention with regard to computer systems are highlighted.

The selection and evaluation of computer equipment is a project that will take time and needs careful management. A time-scale should be established at the outset of the project. The main steps in the project are:

1. Definition of objectives
2. Exploring the options
3. Design a system
4. Implementation
5. Evaluation and maintenance.

Definition of objectives

Decide what you want the system to do and identify priorities. Is word processing the main application, or database creation or numerical analysis through spreadsheets? Are there any special features required in, say, the database application, such as the need to store variable-length data in variable-length fields. The objectives can usefully be summarised in a short document for future reference.

Exploring the options

Discover which systems, including hardware and software, are on the market. Examine the features of the various systems, paying particular attention to price and compatibility. It may take a while to identify the critical features that need to be compared between one system and another. Information can be garnered from a variety of sources. Introductory textbooks, glossaries and training courses may help you to find your way through the jungle of terminology. Once you understand enough of the language to converse with others, visits to exhibitions, suppliers and demonstrations can prove fruitful. Avoid staring in a bemused trance at a screen! Think of questions and participate in the demonstration. Discuss how you expect to use the system. Be prepared to show your ignorance in the interests of getting to the bottom of how things work and the differences between systems. It is the supplier's job to explain the equipment in terms that are comprehensible to the average business user. Read reviews and overviews in the business and computing press, and identify questions to ask suppliers. Finally, talk to other business users who have similar computing requirements to your own. Computer horror stories are usually exchanged with pleasure; learn from this gossip.

At the end of this stage, the document which was written for the first stage should be refined, to produce a more specific requirements specification. Although for small businesses this need only be a short document, it should identify priorities and specify the key features. The production of the requirements specification also creates a breathing space during which the owner/manager can distance himself from salesmanship and reflect.

Design a system

Armed with information on the systems on the market and your requirements, some likely system configurations can be identified. Now is the time to return to the suppliers and examine these potential systems in more depth. Make sure that all parts of the system are compatible with one another. Participate in another round of demonstrations and make in-depth analyses of systems. When you are satisfied that you have identified the best solution, write out a list of all the hardware and software components, and then get an expert, such as the supplier, to check that you have not overlooked anything, such as cables and extra boards. Place the order with the supplier that is offering the cheapest deal on the package that you want to acquire.

Implementation

Once the order is placed, delivery may be immediate or take one or two months, although with some particularly popular models delivery times of three or four months are not unknown. Now is the time to finalise plans for the implementation of the system. Try to take delivery of the complete package at one time, unless a subset is available which will allow you to set up a pilot system.

Implementation starts with the installation of hardware and software, followed by tests to ensure that the complete system is working as it should. These tests are likely to start with trial runs and the establishment of test databases, as well as standard documents for a word processor. Do not forget to try to get data out of a database as well as to put it in. Another facet of implementaton is the establishment of databases and/or spreadsheets, and the transfer of data from existing computer systems or manual systems.

Training runs throughout the implementation of a system. The person responsible for the system may need to attend external training courses. Although these can be expensive, their cost is usually recouped in time saved. Any other users need to be kept generally aware of developments, and, prior to being called upon to use the system, they need some kind of in-house or external training, as well as time to acclimatise themselves to the new system. User training needs to be supported by documentation. Where there are only one or two users, the supplier's documentation may be adequate, but with larger user groups, an in-house user manual might prove more accessible and could be used to summarise in-house practices, such as the storage of files on disks, entry of new records and how to close a session.

Evaluation and maintenance

Initial evaluation should check that the system is meeting its objectives and doing the jobs for which it was intended.

A computer system should run for a number of years, say five, with appropriate maintenance and occasional minor upgrades. Maintenance contracts are highly recommended for hardware and, if available, software. Regular, possibly annual, evaluation of the system should ensure that it continues to fulfil its objectives and will help to identify any shortcomings before they become critical. The organisation will probably outgrow the system eventually and it may be desirable to take advantage of technological advances, so a replacement system will need to be sought. But the next time, you will have some experience upon which to build.

Running the computer system

In general, the running of the computer system should be treated like any other item of electrical equipment. Keep it clean and free from dust, don't spill anything on it and don't run it for so long that it overheats.

Security is principally a consideration when a number of people have access to a system. Security needs to be considered in relation to access to hardware, software and data. Arrangements must ensure that none of these is lost, stolen or damaged. In a small installation, the most common problem is the accidental deletion or loss of software and/or data. To avoid this, do not let other people fiddle with the system (even experts), unless they understand the way that the specific system has been set up, and always keep at least two copies of all software and data. If possible, keep a master copy of software locked in a different room, and save and make back-up copies at regular intervals. Everybody has inadvertently lost some data at some time, so put it down to experience the first time that you do something careless, but try not to repeat the experience too often.

Computers and health

There has been some adverse publicity centred on the effects on health of working with VDUs. Concern has been expressed in relation to pregnancy, epilepsy, radiation, eye-strain, facial dermatitis, tenosynovitis, posture problems and stress. The owner/manager should be aware that problems may occur in individual cases, although evidence from research has failed to prove any detrimental effect of working with VDUs. Any problems can be significantly alleviated by the provision of adequate working conditions with ergonomically designed workstations, suitable lighting and, most importantly, adequate rest periods for operators. No one should work at a VDU for extended periods without a break.

Data protection

All computer users should be conversant with the basic principles of data protection. The Data Protection Act 1984 establishes rights for individuals to have access to their own personal data held on computer files. This means that you need to consider carefully any data about people that is held on computer files. The Act embodies the following principles:

1. Data must be obtained fairly and lawfully.
2. Data must only be held for registered and lawful purposes. Data users must register the personal data that they hold with the Data Protection Registrar.

3. Data must only be used and disclosed for the purposes registered.
4. Data must be adequate, relevant and not excessive for its purpose, and must be kept up to date.
5. Data must not be held for longer than is necessary.
6. Individuals must be allowed access to data about themselves at reasonable intervals and without undue expense, and they must be provided with a copy of it in an intelligible form. Where appropriate, data must be corrected or erased.
7. Data users must take security measures to prevent unauthorised access, disclosure, alteration or destruction of personal data, and against its accidental loss or destruction.
8. The individual or data subject has certain rights and may seek a court order to enforce access to data, and may seek compensation for damage and distress.

If all this sounds too complex, then it is worth noting that the Data Protection Act does not cover manual files, and small-scale files containing personal data may be more easily stored on paper.

Summary

The paperless office is not yet a reality, but a computer can make a significant contribution to office efficiency. Priority should be accorded to the identification of a hardware and software configuration that matches the requirements of your business application.

5

Communication and the Office

Options for communication

Good communication is essential to effective management and relations with customers. It is at the heart of all office activities and can consume considerable resources in both time and money. The office is concerned with receiving, processing, storing and transmitting information which comes into the business in the form of communications from customers, suppliers, official bodies and other sources. Information is also despatched *from* the office. Communications media include letters and business correspondence, leaflets, telephone, facsimile transmission, meetings, electronic mail and computer networks.

This chapter reviews the different communications media. In a business environment, the options for communication do not exist in isolation. It is important to select the most appropriate medium for a given purpose. Usually, a choice between, say, letter, fax or telephone call will be made instantaneously. It may be worth while to pause and consider the factors that should influence the decision to use a particular medium for the communication of a given piece of informaton. Appropriate criteria are:

1. *Efficiency*, or the quickest and least time-consuming medium. A letter will be more efficient than a telephone call if the line is always engaged, but if the recipient is available at the end of a telephone line, a telephone call may eliminate the cost of lengthy correspondence. Often,

a telephone call can be used to clarify a situation, and a letter sent to confirm the arrangements that have been agreed verbally.

2. *Economy* is closely linked with efficiency, because time is money, but the unit cost of each communication should also be considered.

3. *Speed*, particularly where there is some urgency and a quick response is desirable. Facsimile transmission is often used as a substitute for postal services when speed is essential.

4. *Distance*. Whether the communication is internal or external, local, regional, national or international can affect costs and efficiency.

5. *Impressions and impact conveyed* to the recipient by the chosen medium of communication.

6. *Records*. The need to keep a formal record of certain transactions may lead to their being transmitted as letters.

All businesses use a range of communications media and are continually selecting the appropriate medium for a specific type of communication. Time and money can be saved, and image enhanced by appropriate selection.

Written communication

Written communication is a central function of offices. The following list outlines some of the common types of written communication and divides them into three categories: internal to the organisation, external to clients and customers, and external to the wider environment.

Internal
- Memoranda (memos)
- Reports
- Notices
- Agendas
- Minutes
- Contracts
- Handbooks

- Manuals
- Job descriptions
- Job specifications.

External to clients/customers
- Letters
- Circulars
- Price lists
- Publicity leaflets
- Estimates
- Quotations
- Orders
- Delivery notes
- Invoices
- Debit notes
- Credit notes
- Statements
- Export documents.

External to the wider environment
- Reports
- Notices
- Official forms
- Press releases
- Advertisements
- Publicity leaflets
- Articles
- Application forms
- Job specifications.

These different documents have different characteristics in terms of style, contents and structure. Checklist 5.1 lists some of the features that might be considered in drafting a written communication. If you have not had much experience of producing good written business English, it is essential to polish these skills, or employ a secretary to help. The business will be judged on the quality of its written communication and may fail if leaflets, letters, publicity and press releases, which are central to generating business, are not well written.

Checklist 5.1 *What to consider in preparing written communications*

1. Purpose.
2. Addressee.
3. Style and level of formality.
4. Structure, especially for long documents such as reports, where sections with headings and numbering are useful.
5. Spelling, grammar and puncutation need to be checked.
6. Enclosures.
7. Nature of reply expected, and when.
8. Confidentiality.
9. Impact desired.
10. Content, and whether all points have been covered clearly.

Business stationery

Many written communications will be recorded on business stationery, and such communications are the chief means of communication with customers. Stationery also forms the basis of documents that are retained for internal records. The main kinds of business stationery used in most businesses are:

- letterheads
- continuation pages for lengthy correspondence
- compliments slips
- business cards
- envelopes
- orders
- invoices
- credit notes
- statements
- adhesive labels.

Letterheads and all other business documents must comply with the Business Names Act 1985. They must show, legibly, the name of the sole trader, the partners or the corporate name

103

of the company, and an address for each person so named. To facilitate effective communication, stationery should show:

• name
• address, including postcode
• telephone number, including the code of the local exchange
• any fax and telex numbers
• a logo (if the business has one)
• VAT registration number (if applicable).

Careful control of *letterheads* should be exercised, since correspondence on printed letterhead can constitute a contractual agreement between the business and the addressee, and the consequences of the misuse of letterheads may be serious.

Compliments slips are useful for short communications, and for enclosing with publicity to indicate the source of the enclosed documents.

Business cards can be given to contacts as a reminder of your name, address and telephone number. They are often retained by the recipient until the time when your services might be required.

Both compliments slips and business cards should show similar information to that on the letterhead, and may also be used to convey a brief advertising message. Design for maximum impact. Business cards should also carry an individual's name and position.

Envelopes will be needed in at least two or three different sizes. Envelopes can be plain or, for a more personalised image, at a greater cost, printed with the name of the business. Printed envelopes must be made of good quality paper and have a logo or similar on the front, and name, address, telephone number etc on the back flap. Alternatively, the business name and address can be printed by the franking machine, which is much cheaper than pre-printing.

Invoices are made out whenever goods or services are supplied by one person to another. They constitute a contract, so their content should be carefully considered. They are also tax invoices for the purposes of VAT, for those who are registered, and must, by law, be retained for six years as evidence for inspection by Customs and Excise.

Invoices are often multi-copy documents, with say, three, four, five or six parts. The four copies in a typical four-part invoice are usually used thus:

1. The top copy is sent by post to the customer as a notification that the order is in hand and will be delivered shortly. This copy is used by the customer for input tax purposes and forms the source of bookkeeping records for the creditor's ledger.
2. The second copy is retained by the supplier and used to debit the customer's account. It acts as the supplier's copy for output tax records for VAT purposes.
3. The third copy, or *delivery note*, is used to obtain a signature for the goods on delivery. It will not show the value of the consignment.
4. The fourth copy, or *advice note*, is packed with the goods to notify the recipient of the contents. This copy also describes the goods and does not show their value.

An invoice must record the following data:

- names and addresses of both parties to the supply
- the date of the transaction, which will also be the tax point from which taxation will be taken into account for VAT purposes
- details of the supply, including a description of the supply, the quantity, unit price, total value and classification for VAT purposes
- the terms under which the supply is made.

Credit notes are made out whenever one person returns goods to another, or makes an allowance to a customer for some reason. Credit notes usually cancel either part or all of an earlier invoice. The top copy goes to the customer and becomes a VAT document. The second copy is retained for the supplier's accounting records.

A *debit note* may be made out by a supplier when the purchaser was undercharged on the invoice.

Statements. When a customer is given credit, that is, a period of time in which to pay, it is usual for the trader not to be paid on delivery, but rather when a statement of account is rendered. When a large number of transactions is being processed, a statement of account may be rendered at, for instance, the end of each month.

How to obtain stationery

Business stationery may be obtained at competitive prices from local print shops. Yellow Pages lists local outlets. These agencies will print letterheads, envelopes, business cards, documents, brochures, circular letters, leaflets, publicity and other advertising material. Business forms may also be designed on a computer system, and the data input into the form each time a document is printed, such as when an invoice is output from the computer system.

Sizes of paper and envelopes should be compatible. The commonly used sizes are as follows:

Paper
A3   297 mm × 420 mm
A4   210 mm × 297 mm
A5   148 mm × 210 mm
A6   105 mm × 148 mm

Envelopes
C3   324 mm × 458 mm
C4   229 mm × 324 mm
C5   162 mm × 229 mm
C6   114 mm × 162 mm
B4   250 mm × 353 mm
B5   176 mm × 250 mm
B6   125 mm × 176 mm

Mail handling systems

While the small office can operate with simple procedures for handling incoming and outgoing mail, these procedures must be efficient and effective. One advantage of the small organisation is that all mail will probably be dealt with by one or two people, who will therefore have a good understanding of the procedures for dealing with different types of mail, such as orders, complaints and other activities. In a large organisation, this is likely to be carried out by departments or addressees within departments.

Mail inwards

The following points should be borne in mind when processing incoming mail:

1. Start by sorting the mail into categories according to addressee, where mail comes addressed to more than one person. Then sort the mail into printed paper and packages, private, personal and confidential, and other.
2. Open all letters with a letter opener and remove the contents, checking that all contents have been taken out of the envelope. Keep the envelope and attach it to the correspondence if it has taken a long time to reach you or there is no sender's address on the enclosure(s).
3. Check that all enclosures that are indicated have been included and log any omissions. Attach enclosures to the main letter. Any letter containing cheques or other remittances should be carefully checked to ensure that the contents agree with any invoice or remittance advice note. A record book may be kept for recording registered letters, and even remittances in a very small business.
4. Make any copies necessary for anyone else, or files. Send any copies on circulation with appropriate routing slips attached.

Mail outwards

To make effective use of postal services, it is important to be aware of the services available and any relevant time-scales.

The times of last collection are crucial, as they may determine work flow in the office earlier in the day.

The *Post Office Guide* is useful and all post offices issue free leaflets about postal rates. Basically, postal services can been divided into letter post, parcel post and, for overseas mail, printed paper rate. Also, a range of other miscellaneous services such as Datapost, Admail, and Redirected Mail can be exploited.

Basic postal equipment is cheap and valuable. Letter and parcel weighing scales, roller and sponge dampers, wrapping paper and adhesive tape are a basic kit. Stamps should be bought in sheets; if the volume of mail is substantial, a franking machine can be used.

Meetings

Meetings are a major means of communication. Meetings may be among staff within an organisation, or with customers or other outsiders. Meetings will vary in their objectives and their level of formality, but it is always wise to identify the objectives of a meeting at the planning stage, and to share these objectives with all the participants.

In general, meetings may be convened for one of the following purposes:

- to provide information to a group of people
- to discuss ideas and proposals and formulate future plans, involving creative thinking and decision-making
- to solve problems
- to co-ordinate activities, with members reporting on progress
- to share knowledge and thus share facts
- to unite a team
- to encourage participation and involvement
- to fulfil a statutory obligation.

Committees of various kinds are common in large organisations, and small business managers are more likely to encounter committees in their dealings with such organisations than within their own organisations. It is important to identify the responsibility and status of a committee, and, to establish whether the committee can authorise or make recommendations concerning expenditure.

All meetings, however large or small, formal or informal, depend on a Chairman for their effectiveness. The Chairman has responsibilities in completing tasks outside the meeting, conducting the meeting and controlling other members. Even in a meeting of only three or four people, someone needs to take the initiative in defining its objectives, deciding how, when and why the meeting should be held, controlling the issues to be discussed and ensuring that action is agreed. Other participants should be active. They should have studied the agenda and the paperwork, and:

- if they are representatives, have discussed the issues with others
- be prepared to explore their own and others' views in order to reach a consensus
- be conversant with meetings procedure
- be prepared to become involved and take follow-up action
- be prepared to report back to colleagues.

Most meetings, however informal, generate some paperwork. As a basic minimum, a meeting is likely to require the following:

1. *A notice* of the *meeting*, giving the type of meeting, day, time, place and name, description and contact point of the convenor.
2. *An agenda*, which may incorporate a notice of the meeting, is essentially a list of things to be done. This is usually accompanied by any papers necessary to support discussion of the agenda items, and these need to be circulated in sufficient time for the members to read them. There may also be a more detailed chairman's agenda.
3. *Minutes*, which record what takes place at a meeting. They are consulted at subsequent meetings for reference, and should also be used between meetings to trigger actions.

4. *Other documents*, which may include proposals, reports of working groups, documents for discussion, statistics, copies of correspondence, accounts and job applications.

Telephone systems

Telephones are central to communication with customers, suppliers, agents and others. Good telephone links are vital. There is a wide range of options for telephone systems, and the larger the organisation the more complex the system. The emphasis here is on arrangements that are appropriate for the smaller business.

Customers must be able to contact your business by telephone whenever they want. The telephone system must have sufficient capacity to handle the anticipated volume of calls, and, in the absence of anyone to receive a call, an answer phone is invaluable.

All people who might answer the telephone, whether they be employees, family or friends, should be trained in taking messages. Greet the caller with the name of the business, followed by 'May I help you?'. Always take the name, number and a brief description of the topic, and any other special notes such as urgency or times to call back, as well as the date and time of the call. Finally, repeat back the message to the caller to check the accuracy of the message.

If the business takes a large number of telephone orders, a separate line could be allocated for this purpose, possibly manned by an experienced order clerk.

Telephone equipment

Telephone equipment is available from a number of manufacturers. Choose a 'British Telecom Approved' instrument. This designation means that the equipment has been tested and found to be compatible with British Telecom lines. Such telephones may be plugged into any telephone socket.

Many telephones offer a memory, which stores numbers that can be retrieved for dialling. Some give a visual display and others have a 24-hour clock. The choice depends on preferences and how much you are prepared to spend.

In addition to the standard telephone, specialised instruments are also available.

Loudspeaking telephones

The loudspeaking telephone does not need to be held, thus permitting the user to do other things with his hands during a conversation, such as riffle through papers. Calls can be dialled or concluded with a single finger.

Videophones

Videophones connect the telephone to a television monitor, so that callers can see each other. These are currently too expensive for everyday use.

Cordless telephones

Cordless telephones do not have a cable or cord link, but operate by radio transmission between the handset and a base unit. Power for the handset is provided by batteries which are recharged when the handset is replaced on the base. The base unit is powered via a transformer connected to the mains electricity, and as well as recharging the handset, also announces the calls. The handset may be carried up to 100 to 200 metres from the base unit, which may be convenient when it is necessary to move about within a building or restricted area, leaving the office unattended. Cordless telephones usually also offer personal paging, automatic redialling and an in-built security code.

Cellular telephones

Cellular telephones are mobile telephones intended for use on the move. Two networks operate in the UK; Cellnet (a joint venture between British Telecom and Securicor) and Vodaphone (offered by Racal). Most equipment is compatible with both networks.

There are three basic types of cellular telephone:

1. *Mobiles* for use in cars, which are permanently installed in a motor vehicle.

2. *Portables* for use anywhere, which rely upon a rechargeable battery.
3. *Transportables*, which are larger and suitable for use as car telephones or elsewhere.

The use of a cellular telephone should not be allowed to interfere with driving. There are provisions concerning the use of such telephones in the Highway Code, and safety must always come first.

Starting with telephones

What kind of telephone configuration is essential when a small business is first established? The array of handsets and exchanges on the market can be confusing. The basic minimum is probably:

*   a good basic telephone
*   a telephone answering machine
*   a cordless telephone, for additional flexibility.

This basic system can be expanded as the business grows by adding additional handsets and considering the options for switching systems and exchanges.

Making a telephone call

A telephone call should be planned and have a structure. Before making the call, decide who you want to talk to and make sure that you have their name and extension. Prepare a list of points to discuss, and collect any appropriate papers, then:

1. Dial the number carefully. Wrong numbers irritate both you and the recipient.
2. Be able to identify tones, such as the dialling tone, the ringing tone, the engaged tone and the unobtainable tone.
3. When there is an answer, say who you are and who you represent (for example: John Brown, Gloucester Glazing), and to whom you wish to speak. Give the person's

extension number if you know it; if you do not, find out
the extension number for future calls.

4. If you have to leave a message, leave your name, the
   name of your organisation and the telephone number on
   which you can be contacted, indicate times when you are
   available, and whether you wish to be called back, or
   whether you will call back later. Also indicate the
   urgency of your business.

5. If the subject of your enquiry may be handled by more
   than one person, accept a response from an appropriate
   substitute for the original contact, if this wastes less time.
   If your call is handled by another person, ensure that you
   record that person's name and extension number for
   future reference.

6. During the call, make sure that all the points that you
   planned to cover have been raised and satisfactorily
   resolved.

7. Remember that telephone calls cost most before 1 pm.
   Afternoon calls cost less, and evening calls after 6 pm are
   cheaper still.

Exchanges and switching systems

Once the business grows to the stage where more than one telephone is required, exchanges, or at the very least switching
systems, need to be considered. Larger businesses have
exchanges or switchboards, but these need to be manned by a
switchboard operator or a telephonist. (The duties of a
telephonist and receptionist are often carried out by one person.) The growing business is unlikely to be able to justify a
full-time switchboard operator, and may benefit from a key
system.

A key system does not require an operator. Any extension
user may answer incoming calls and transfer them to other
extensions as required. Each telephone handset in the system
has keys for each of the extensions. Lights indicate when
extensions are engaged. A small system of this kind may have
two lines and up to four extensions.

Larger organisations merit a switchboard or Private Branch

Exchange (PABX). Operators answer and route all incoming calls. Extension users can dial their own outgoing calls, unless this facility is deliberately barred. Larger organisations usually also have an internal telephone system to facilitate communication between members of staff.

Both PABX and key systems offer a bewildering array of special features designed to aid effective communication. Some common features are:

1. *Call back*, which allows a user who has dialled an extension, and found it to be engaged, to replace the handset and then to reactivate the call later, merely by lifting the handset.
2. *Abbreviated dialling*, so that frequently called numbers can be dialled just by keying in a code, of say, two digits.
3. *Call barring*, which restricts the placing of certain categories of call, such as long distance or international calls.
4. *Call diversion*, where a user can direct his calls to another extension.
5. *Call queuing.*
6. *Call re-routing*, so that if the telephone is not answered after a given number of rings, the call will automatically re-route to another pre-selected extension.
7. *Last number recall*, so that the last number called can be automatically redialled.
8. *Waiting return*, where incoming calls are sent back to the switchboard if the call is not answered within a specified time.

Telephone systems are also available that have a number of special features to assist the disabled (including those with speech, visual and mobility impairment), such as convenient height sockets and aids for deaf people.

British Telecom offer a range of telephone services. These include directory enquiries, the speaking clock, alarm calls, road conditions reports, weather forecasts and the *Financial Times* share index service. Also, services such as Freefone, for which callers incur no charge, emergency 999 calls, card phones, transfer charge calls, and calls to ships at sea and air-craft may all be of interest. For further details of these and other services available from British Telecom, consult British Telecom literature, including phone books and Yellow Pages.

Answering machines

Like other telephone equipment, answering machines can be purchased or rented. They operate from a special socket which allows the answering machine access to the telephone network, without interfering with the telephone. When switched to 'Answer', the machine responds to incoming calls by accepting the call and playing a pre-recorded announcement. When using an answering machine it is useful to record a brief message at the end of the recorded messages, to act as a marker before replaying the messages. Answering machines are not only devices for receiving messages; they also confirm who has been trying to contact you.

Answering machines can be grouped into three categories:

1. Those that answer only, and do not record.
2. Those that answer and record.
3. Those that form a combined telephone and answering machine, some of which have remote control.

In addition to the basic function of recording messages, some answering machines also offer the following additional features:

1. Remote control, so that a user can contact his own machine and listen to any messages. The machine is activated either by a bleeper or voice.
2. Recording of any telephone conversation, so that it can be reviewed or transcribed later.
3. Call screening and monitoring, so that the user can listen to messages as they are being recorded, decide whether to take a call and intercept as appropriate.

Personal preference will dictate which type of machine should be acquired.

Radio-paging machines

Radio paging is useful when you need to be contacted or paged across wide areas. There are three kinds of system:

1. *Tone-only pagers*, which beep only, and the user then has to dial the relevant telephone number from a normal telephone. The call is then switched automatically to a transmitter network operated by the supplier and is subsequently relayed to the user via radio wave. Silent pagers where vibration replaces the tone are also available.
2. *Display systems*, which have a small light-emitting diode (LED) which can display brief messages. These messages may be purely numeric, such as a telephone number, or alpha-numeric, capable of displaying limited written information.
3. *Voice systems*, which operate only on UHF frequency and are therefore less useful over a wide area. Since they operate one way only, they have been superseded by the cellular telephone.

Telex and teletex

Telex and teletex are means of sending messages. Their relevance may be limited for the small business, but they are options that may need to be explored.

Telex is the oldest form of electronic mail. Telex machines are connected to the telex network. Data may be input at one machine and output as a print-out at another machine in the network. Electronic telex machines are similar to word processors, and, indeed, upgraded memory typewriters or adapted microcomputers can be used as telex machines. The great attraction of telex is that the service will operate whether or not the receiving machine is manned, provided that it is switched on and fitted with paper. Messages are printed out and can be picked up by the recipient later.

A small business may find that the volume of telex messages is insufficient to justify in-house equipment. Instead, an electronic mail or telex bureau may be employed to send and receive messages. The bureau communicates these messsages to you over the telephone or via another electronic mail system.

Teletex transmits and receives mail via the telephone network, using either the Public Switched Telephone Network (PSTN) or British Telecom's Packet Switch Stream. While teletex uses normal telephone lines, telex necessitates the rental of separate lines, which are more expensive than normal telephone lines. Teletex is a memory-to-memory system so that the final print quality is a function of the output printer. Whereas telex operates only in upper-case, teletex can produce letter-quality documents. Teletex is also easier to operate and safeguard features are built in, including a log of what happens to every call. Teletex can be linked with telex, so that the user can communicate with terminals on the international telex network. Equipment is, however, still rather expensive, and teletex has yet to take off in a big way.

Electronic mail

The term 'electronic mail' may refer to a wide range of electronic data transmission services, but is most often applied to services offered by electronic mail bureaux, such as British Telecom's Telecom Gold, or used to describe an organisation's internal mailbox system operated via its own computer.

Bureaux services are most likely to be relevant to the small business. Electronic mail bureaux are based on large central computers whose storage is allocated as 'mailboxes'. Electronic mail offers a general message facility. The user can transmit and receive messages, set up a record-keeping system, manage appointments, contact telex subscribers, receive telex messages and page the mailbox when out of the office.

Facsimile transmission (fax)

Facsimile machines transmit an exact copy (facsimile) of a document, over telephone networks, to another facsimile machine. Facsimile transmission is a very attractive option for transmitting documents. A major advantage over telex is that the document is scanned into the machine, so does not need to be rekeyed; thus, time is saved and accuracy improved. In addition, drawings can also be transmitted.

When a document is fed into a fax machine, it is scanned and the information is encoded into a series of electrical pulses, which are then sent down the telephone line. At the other end, the image is reconstructed and printed. One reason for the success of fax is that machines do not need to be of the same make to communicate with one another, provided that they conform to the industry standard groups established by the CCITT.

There are four groups of fax machine. The main distinction between the machines in the different groups is the transmission speed. If two machines are communicating with one another, the transmission takes place at the speed of the slower machine. Most machines currently in use are Group 3. Group 4 are the most sophisticated machines and will operate with digital telephone lines.

In addition to transmission speed, a number of other features of fax machines vary. These are:

1. *Dialling*, such as automatic redialling for numbers that were engaged.
2. *Reduction and enlargement*. Most machines handle A4 size only. Reduction facilities are useful for handling drawings and computer print-out. Enlargement can improve the quality of transmission of small documents with poor definition.
3. *Printing*. Most machines employ thermal printing using heat-sensitive paper, but there is a trend towards plain-paper printers, and more recently, laser printers.
4. *Output quality*. Output from fax machines has always been poorer than that available from a good photocopier, but quality is improving. The sharpness of the image is determined by the resolution of the image transmitted; the higher the resolution the better the image. Also, the effectiveness of the scanner in distinguishing black and white influences image quality, and particular problems can arise with documents containing half-tones or shades of grey.
5. *Errors*. Line interference can distort the image or lose part

of the image. Machines have an automatic cut-off when a certain level of image corruption is reached (about 15 per cent), but it is difficult to detect the level of corruption from the transmitter's end. The only options are to retransmit the complete document or to wait for the receiver to notify you of any problems.

6. *Memory*. Memory may be available for auto-dialling and to store documents on random access memory (RAM) or hard disk. Memory is useful for store-and-forward, and broadcasting to many users, since in both instances it is possible to separate the creation of the message from its transmission.

The future of fax looks promising. More plain-paper copier machines, Group 4 machines, computer links with VDU display, and increases in transmission speeds, are likely.

Intelpost is the Post Office's fax service. Documents can be handed in at designated post offices for transmission to another centre. At the destination, the document is collected or messenger delivery arranged.

Courier services

A number of courier services offer quick and speedy transmission of documents. The options include:

1. *Special messenger services*, which take documents and small packages from one location to another at high speed.
2. *National courier services*, which guarantee delivery within the country the next day, or the same day, such as the Royal Mail's Datapost, Securicor, Red Star (from British Rail) and Roadline (part of National Freight).
3. *Overseas document delivery services*, which use air courier services. Delivery ranges from next day to third day. Services are the Royal Mail's International Datapost, Express Air Ltd, Transworld Couriers, World Courier (UK) Ltd and many other companies.

Names are found in Yellow Pages under 'Courier services' and 'Delivery and collection services'.

Networks

As long as your business is small and your communication needs are modest, you will be able to avoid any but the merest contact with networks. Networks appear in two guises: external telecommunications networks, such as those operated by British Telecom, and internal networks, usually in the form of local area networks, or possibly wide area networks.

Many of the services that have been discussed earlier in this chapter rely upon external telecommunications networks. Networks support telephones, telex and facsimile transmission. Special networks for data transmission, as opposed to voice transmission, are available both nationally and internationally. For example, your microcomputer or terminal can communicate with a computer elsewhere in the world through British Telecom's Packet Switch Stream Service (PSS), and then through International Packet Switch Stream (IPSS). Telecommunications network suppliers are continually upgrading services in these areas, so if you have a requirement for large-scale data transmission, it is worth contacting the major suppliers and enquiring about their current services and schedule of charges.

Local area networks are used within an organisation to link computers together. Once your business has acquired and is using about four to six machines, you may wish to investigate the potential of local area networks. Local area networks allow users to communicate with one another and to share facilities such as a printer or storage, or a database. There are a number of issues to consider when looking at local area networks, including:

1. The services required and the benefits expected
2. The kind of application (eg office automation only or CAD, sales etc also)
3. Network architecture
4. Network topology
5. Serving distance or distance covered by the network
6. Cabling link and its physical form
7. Access methods to the network
8. Other design criteria such as the number of nodes, central control, power requirements

9. Terminals and their type
10. Financial aspects, including capital, rentals, maintenance and operating costs.

If the checklist above introduces too much unfamiliar jargon, it should at least serve to demonstrate that it is necessary to consult an expert when considering networks.

Summary

The office is the heart of the communication in a small business. There are a number of communications media that can be used to transmit documents and verbal exchanges. It is important to match the medium to the circumstances and to use the media appropriately.

6
Records Management

Why do you need records and a filing system?

Every organisation, however small, generates and receives documents such as letters, invoices, reports, information leaflets and newspaper cuttings. A filing system keeps these documents in order so that they can be retrieved efficiently and effectively.

The golden rule is to put documents away once they have been dealt with. If the matter to which the documents relate is still in progress, then documents can be filed in a pending file. Time expended in the design and maintenance of a records management or filing system will eliminate a lot of time spent searching for lost documents. Just one lost document can cost of lot of time, so be meticulous with your filing system from the start. In the extreme, without effective document retrieval, management decisions will be less well informed and judgement may be impaired. The discipline of effective filing and organisation of records needs to become a habit, both for the business owner/manager and his office staff.

Files

A file is a collection of letters or documents dealing with one organisation, person, area or subject. Files may hold paper documents, or may be computer-based. Database and word-processing software were introduced in Chapter 4; these types of software, like others, can be used to create and maintain computer-based files. The emphasis in this chapter is on paper-based systems, but many of the principles outlined here can also be translated to the maintenance of computer-based files.

While you must be disciplined about filing documents, not all documents need to be filed. Examine all documents and identify those that do not merit long-term retention. Throw papers away when they have served their purpose. Do not file in the main filing system documents that are:

- unimportant, or whose message has been read and dealt with; these can go straight into the waste-paper bin
- useful for only a short period; these can be placed in temporary or working folders, then removed to more permanent storage or the bin, later
- readily obtainable from some other source.

Filing systems

The different physical systems for holding documents in files include:

1. *Vertical suspension system*s, in which files are put in pockets hung from runners in desks, cabinets or trolleys. Identification tabs are located at the top, and the insertion and retrieval of files is from the top. Such systems are tidy and offer documents good protection from fire and dust. Papers can be inserted without files being removed from the system. Such systems do, however, occupy a lot of floor space, and space must be allowed for pulling out the runner housing. There is a tendency to overfill pockets, because the insertion of a large quantity of new material requires a lot of shuffling of files between the runner housings.

2. *Lateral filing system*s, which are banks of suspended files, or files on shelves that are taller than vertical suspension systems. With such a system, it is possible to store many more files per square metre of floor space. In addition, a

large number of files can be viewed at a glance and several people can access files simultaneously. Care must be exercised in labelling files so that labels on high files can be viewed from floor level. Files are prone to become dusty due to the large opening, and it may be difficult to reach and pull out files from a high position.

Multi-purpose cabinets may suit the small business. These combine, in one cabinet, some vertical and some lateral filing, as well as filing for floppy disks, computer print-out and card indexes.

3. *Rotary systems*, in which files are suspended as in lateral filing, but radiating out from a central revolving pillar. There are usually several tiers, each of which can revolve independently. Rotary systems may hold lever arch files or index cards.

4. *Horizontal filing* which is specialist filing for maps, plans and drawings. Documents are stored in shallow drawers one on top of another. They take up a lot of space and documents need to be handled excessively in retrieval, thereby making them vulnerable to damage.

5. *Chest plan filing*, which is a more satisfactory solution for storing maps, charts and plans. Documents are separated by dividers and suspended from a rail or clip, or stand free between dividers. Various sizes are available, and the cabinets are mobile and fireproof.

6. *Mobile systems*, which are large multi-tiered filing cabinets on floor tracks with vertical or lateral suspension filing that can be opened or closed for access. The term 'mobile systems' may also be used to refer to simple mobile file units which consist of single drawers placed on trolleys.

7. *Binders and files*, which may be hung in appropriate units or arranged on shelves. Options include loose-leaf binders, box files, lever arch files and concertina files. Such devices facilitate the grouping together of a relatively large number of related documents.

8. *Microform storage*. Documents can be stored as microforms. Microforms are particularly valuable where space is at a premium, since they occupy only 2 per cent of the space of equivalent paper files. Microforms can be stored

as roll film, jackets, microfiche, aperture cards and COM (computer output microfilm) fiche. Microform is more durable than paper and easy to access. It is also easy to produce a hard copy of stored documents. The chief drawbacks are the equipment that is required to prepare and read the microforms, in the form of cameras, duplicators, readers and printers, and the time taken in filming and indexing documents.

9. *Computer-based storage.* Many organisations build up significant files on floppy and hard disks. Computer-based files are particularly appropriate for customers' and suppliers' accounts, stock control records, wages records, production planning, costing and budgetary control, and other statistical information for mangement control. Optical disks are capable of storing large quantities of data; as these become better established, they are likely to be used both for storing current documents and for archives. Computer-based files have two distinct advantages over paper-based files: many people can have access simultaneously and there is no need to trace files. In addition, with appropriate software, indexing can be automatic.

A policy for records management

Filing and records management systems should be designed, not just allowed to grow. Decisions concerning the use of such a system and access to it should be made. Both the initial establishment of a system and the continuing development of the system need to be controlled. The following common faults in records management systems have been identified:

1. The wrong system of classification has been adopted
2. Bad organisation and lack of definition of responsibility and authority
3. Untrained and unsuitable staff
4. No established filing procedures, such as new files being created without authority or control
5. No planned schedules for retention or disposal of records
6. Inadequate space and equipment

7. Lack of control over the borrowing of records or their return.

This list summarises those areas that need attention. It also demonstrates that an effective records management system depends on a number of crucial management decisions. Records of borrowing of files may be less important for systems that are only used by one person. Nevertheless, it is quite possible to achieve muddle in a one-person system if the above areas are not given sufficient attention.

There are three different levels of interaction with a records management system:

1. Overall policy decisions concerning what kind of item to file, when to create new files, retention policies etc. Such decisions must be made in full knowledge of the operations that the filing system supports, and are thus best made by the manager, after taking advice.
2. Execution of the policy decisions identified above, such as filing documents, discarding documents and creating new files. Execution may be the responsibility of office staff, although there is no reason why the manager and others should not put documents that they have been using away if this is quick and they can be relied upon to put things in the right place.
3. Using the filing system to extract information, which may be done by anybody in the business or by office staff on behalf of others. Access and security of files needs to be maintained; if many people have direct access to a system, control mechanisms need to be implemented.

Designing a records management system

Any records management system must be tailored to serve the business for which it is to be used. It is therefore important that the filing system be designed locally by someone who understands how the business operates and who appreciates the way in whch the filing system will be used. The factors to be taken into account in the design of a filing system are as follows:

1. Subjects, committees, organisations and areas to be covered
2. Types of document to be included and their characteristics, such as length, origin and character
3. Quantity of literature, both now and for the future
4. Type of storage system
5. Resources of the filing system
6. Users of the system
7. Use, including frequency of use, types of demand and degree of urgency attached to use of the system
8. Personal, group and centralised filing, and the extent of each
9. Security and confidentiality level required for documents
10. Accommodation and office space available, including floor loading, space for examining documents and drawer opening space.

A good filing system is one that takes all the factors into account and exhibits the following features:

1. Compactness, so that it does not take up too much space
2. Accessibility, with ease of filing and extraction of documents
3. Simplicity in operation
4. Security of documents, with possibly varying levels of security for different document types
5. Economy of labour and materials
6. Speedy retrieval
7. Elasticity and capacity for expansion
8. Minimal misfiling
9. Good classification, cross-referencing and indexing
10. Records always filed up to date
11. Control of documents when they have been removed from the system.

All these factors may contribute to a good system, but the basic criterion on which any records management system is judged is *the speed with which documents can be found*.

Basic filing systems

A number of basic systems can be used to arrange files. Table 6.1 lists the key advantages and disadvantages of the most common approaches, such as alphabetical headings, coded classification, and classification based on geographical location and date. Both alphabetical headings and coded classification can be used to arrange files according to their subjects, or according to names of organisations, individuals or committees. Combinations of these various arrangements are likely to be appropriate in any one filing system, but the most simple systems are probably based on alphabetical headings. Above all else, the filing system must meet the requirements of the business. It must accommodate every document that needs to be retained, and, once filed, every document must be easy to find.

Arranging files by subject

Files are commonly arranged according to the subject or topic of the content of documents. Any such system must be derived from the subjects of existing documents and the predicted subjects of future documents. When designing a system based on subjects, it is important to reflect on specificity and the relationships between documents:

- *Specificity*. Should a file be created for all the documents on Materials, or one for each of Glass, Ceramics and Metal? The level of specificity adopted in a filing system must match the requirements of that particular set of documents. The aim is to create files with a reasonable number of documents in them – that is, not too large or too small. This is more difficult to achieve that might be apparent, since the situation is dynamic.
- *Relationships*. Subjects do not stand in isolation but are related to one another. A file on Building Materials may provide some useful information, but a searcher may also wish to consult related files on Bricks, Wood, Glass and Construction Methods. The aim is to group documents that are likely to be frequently used together into one file.

Two divergent approaches are available for organising documents by subject: alphabetical subject labels and classification schemes. Alphabetical subject labels give direct access, in alphabetical sequence, to topics that are labelled with ordinary names, such as Housing, Hospitals. Classification schemes generate codes that can be quoted in documents, but which mean nothing, such as CAR345. Classification schemes are intended to group files on related subjects together. An index is necessary to translate ordinary terms into the codes in the scheme.

Classification schemes

A classification scheme consists of three elements:

1. The schedules in which subjects are listed systematically
2. The coding or notation
3. The alphabetical index.

Indexes and codes are covered later in this chapter.

First priority must be accorded to developing the basic order of subjects, or the schedules. The schedules, or subject list, should exist as a list separate from the files themselves, and should include:

- subjects to cater for all documents covered by the system
- scope for insertion of new subjects and deletion of old subjects
- sufficient subjects to allow all files to be maintained at a manageable size
- subjects listed in a systematic order.

This list of subjects can be generated by working through the following steps:

1. Decide the purpose of the scheme, including its scope, documents to be filed, quantity of material covered, type of system and users, and use.
2. Create a random list of the subjects that need to be included.

Table 6.1 *Types of filing system and their advantages/disadvantages*

Filing system	Advantages	Disadvantages	Examples
Alphabetical headings Documents are filed in accordance with headings that are alphabetical names or subject terms	Documents are grouped by subject or name of company Direct filing and retrieval with no index required Simple and easy to understand	In large systems it can be difficult to find papers Congestion may occur under common names and subjects Documents may get scattered under more than one heading Difficult to forecast space requirements for different letters of the alphabet in expanding systems	Filing of correspondence, contracts and staff records
Coded classification Each document and file is assigned a code and filed in order according to that code	Greater accuracy in filing File number can be used as a reference for correspondence Unlimited expansion possible The index may be used for other purposes, such as a list of business contacts	More time is required in referring to the index prior to filing and retrieval Need to design and maintain the classified system of categories	Filing of sales invoices, contracts and committee minutes

Geographical classificaton

Documents are filed according to their geographical location

Convenient for reference when location is known

Possibility of error when geographical knowledge is weak

An index may be necessary

Geographical location and labels must be known

Filing of customers' orders in sales area order, or correspondence according to town

Chronological classification

Documents are filed in date order; the system is rarely used absolutely, but documents are commonly filed in chronological order inside each folder

Current correspondence can be located easily

Documents are grouped in accordance with the date when they were dealt with, which often has the effect of grouping associated documents together

Incoming and outgoing letters can get separated if files are kept in strict chronological sequence

Chronological filing is rarely appropriate for a complete system since it does not group documents according to topic

3. Group these subjects into related groups.
4. Label the related groups.
5. Adjust the arrangement of subject within the related groups.
6. Append a notation to the list of subjects.
7. Compile an index and a finished list of subjects with attached notation.
8. Do not forget to revise the list as necessary to accommodate new subjects.

Alphabetical subject labels

Alphabetical labels for subjects appear to be more straightforward than classification and are often the first system that a small business might consider. Despite their relative simplicity, there remain some pitfalls that should be avoided. First, terminology may present some problems, such as the following:

- *Synonyms.* Synonyms are terms with the same or similar meaning. Sometimes terms may be regarded as synonyms and all documents associated with any of the terms filed in one file, but on other occasions terms may merit different files. For example, take the two terms Telecommunications and Networks; sometimes these will effectively be the same, while on other occasions documents dealing with these topics will need to be filed separately. Care must be taken to avoid, or, if necessary, arrange appropriately, many files with the same or similar labels.
- *Plurals and singulars.* Some nouns have different connotations in the plural and singular forms, eg Church or Churches. The convention is to use plurals unless there is a good reason not to do so, so that you would use Bricks and not Brick.
- *Multiple-word terms.* Multiple-word terms are terms where two or more words are necessary to name a subject. Examples include: Equal Opportunities, Data Protection, Environment and Conservation, Health and Safety. Direct order is more predictable and is therefore recommended.

Relationships between subjects also need to be handled. Cross-references can be used to link related subjects (see page 135).

It is useful to generate a list of the labels to be used in a filing system. This list shows the topics that are covered and assists in selecting new headings for files. A list of subject labels can be compiled by following these five steps:

1. Decide the purpose of the list, including its scope, documents to be filed, quantity of material covered, type of system and users, and use.
2. Start to list terms by identifying the main areas and examining documents to be covered.
3. Record terms, perhaps one to a record card. Note any comments or cross-references that might be necessary. File terms in alphabetical order. These cards will then form the basis of an index.
4. Check terms and notes, and produce a final version, either on cards or paper, depending on the number of users of the system.
5. Revise the list as necessary.

Codes and coding

The central function of any code is to impose a self-evident order on a set of files. A code should facilitate filing. A unique symbol should be assigned to each separate subject, name, geographical area or file. The coding should not determine the basic sequences of the files, but should be superimposed on a sequence in which the basic order of concepts has already been determined. Codes may be assigned to files arranged in any kind of sequence, but are particularly appropriate for files arranged in a classified sequence according to their subject content.

Since all codes must impose a self-evident order, potential codes must be comprised of the only two character sets whose order is self-evident: numbers and letters. Letters may be upper and lower case. Any other symbols that are introduced into a code (such as ?, < or £) need to have their filing value defined. Codes may be pure or mixed. A pure code uses just numbers or letters, eg 456, 698.56, TIUM. A mixed code uses more than one kind of symbol, eg DA432, C.Pt.1.9.

A good code must be simple, brief and hospitable to new subjects. Expressiveness or the ability to indicate the relationships between subjects might also be welcomed.

Names as file labels

Names of people, companies, local government and government bodies are important as file labels in correspondence files and files of committee papers. Usually, it is fairly clear when a new file needs to be created with a particular name as label, because that person or organisation has started to feature in the transactions of the business. Note that it is normal to file correspondence under the name of departments or companies, and not under the name of the person who wrote the letter.

There are two types of problem that may be encountered in formulating file labels from names:

1. If a person or body has more than one name or an alias, it may not be clear which name to use as the file label.
2. If the name can be presented in more than one form (for instance, as an abbreviation or in full) or is prefixed, the choice of form of name may prove difficult.

In such cases, you must decide which name to use and provide cross-references as appropriate. The following examples outline some common problems:

Name	*File label*
Peter Larkin (or P. Larkin)	Larkin, Peter (or Larkin, P.)
Kevin Henderson Smythe	Henderson Smythe, Kevin
Georges Van Vogt	Van Vogt, Georges
Department of the Environment	Department of the Environment

Name	*File label*
Computer Innovations plc Software Developments, Programming Unit	Computer Innovations Software Developments, Programming Unit
The Royal Society of Chemistry	Royal Society of Chemistry
Chang Lang Wong	Chang Lang Wong
United States of America	USA

A master list of file headings should be maintained, as discussed elsewhere. As well as assisting in the location of lost files, such a master list shows the headings and forms of headings that have already been admitted into the system. Consultation of the list helps to ensure that new headings are established in a style that is consistent with headings already established.

Cross-references

Cross-references assist the user who searches under a different name from that which has been used as the file label. Cross-references help to make a system accessible to the many different people who bring different perspectives and requirements to the records management system, by reminding users of other places where documents may have been filed. Cross-references are necessary in all types of filing sequences, whether based on names, subjects or even codes. In any sequence based on alphabetical headings, cross-references can be incorporated into the main file sequence. Provided that they are visible, they may be recorded on guide cards or the files themselves. In a sequence based on codes, references normally appear in the index.

To be helpful, cross-references must be clear, simple and used sparingly. It is not possible to lay down any criteria as to when references are likely to be necessary, but there is some skill involved in predicting when a reference might serve a useful purpose.

There are two types of reference:

1. *See* references, eg 'Indexing *see* Information retrieval'. *See* references should be used to link two headings where there is nothing stored under the first heading. So, if the reference above was made, this would imply that there were no documents stored under Indexing.
2. *See also* references, eg 'Clinics *see also* Health Centres'. *See also* references should be used to link two headings where there are documents stored under both headings, but where, once the documents stored under the first heading have been consulted, it might be advisable to examine documents under the second heading. *See also* references then link related labels.

Cross-references can be viewed as a means of controlling the number of copies of documents that need to be stored. Ideally, only one copy of each document should be stored in a filing system. Sometimes it is convenient to store a number of copies of, say, a letter in different files, but in general the filing system should not be swollen by additional copies of documents.

Indexes

Indexes are a useful supplement to any filing system and are essential for the filing system that is based on codes. An index may not be necessary for an alphabetical system where it does no more than duplicate the list of file labels recorded on the files. An index serves to:

- indicate the location of specific topics in a coded classification
- locate documents on related topics that have been filed in separate locations.

The index should be a series of entries that lead from the main entry or look-up term to the label under which documents have been stored in the system. For example:

Look-up term	*Index term*
Office telephones	A13(a)
Telephones	A13(a)
Microcomputers	*see* Computers
Environment, Department of	*see* Department of the the Environment

There are a number of physical forms of index:

- book or page index
- card index
- other assorted indexes, such as visible card index, rotary index and strip index
- computer-based index.

Whatever its physical form, the index provides help in retrieving documents from a specific filing systems. Many of the earlier comments in this chapter concerning alphabetical subject labels and names as labels should also be noted in the construction of indexes. The indexing of large collections of documents is a specialised task, and if your index mushrooms beyond your control, it may be time to seek further advice from a professional indexer.

Filing order

A filing order must be established for any labels used in a filing system. Without a recognised filing sequence, the only way to find any specific file is to examine the labels of all the files in the system!

Most labels will be filed according to the self-evident sequence of the labels, which will usually be alphabetically or numerically. Other options are chronological, geographical or a combination of these orders. Refinements will be required on most basic sequences to determine whether John Macmillan's file should be found before or after Eli Mcmillan's file, and to decide the sequence of file labels such as S.A.L.E., SALE, Säle, 3SA's plc, a sale, Sales, Sales Orders, Salesman and Sales, direct.

There are no universally adopted filing practices, but BS 1749 'Recommendations for alphabetical arrangement and the filing order of numerals and symbols' is a useful guide. A simple code of filing rules should be drafted which covers any problems that are likely to be encountered in the given system.

Other considerations

There are a number of other issues associated with records management systems that merit brief mention.

Weeding and retention policies

A filing system needs to be dynamic. Rarely used files should be moved to archival storage, and redundant documents weeded out and discarded. Weeding and retention policies should be established with the support of the manager. Retention periods need to be established for different kinds of document. Retention and weeding policies depend on:

- the relative value of documents, including uniqueness and significance
- existence/availability of other copies
- format in which information must be retained
- legal requirements
- desired speed of retrieval
- space available.

Weeded documents can be shredded. Shredded paper can be recycled. Ensure that confidential documents are destroyed.

Computer files also need weeding. Both floppy disks and hard disks need to be weeded, either by deleting or transferring documents to back-up disks.

Archival storage may be as microfilm, or as long-term paper storage. If documents are to be retained in their original form, they can be transferred to strong fibreboard boxes and stored in a location that is safe from fire, dust, dirt, damp and temperature changes.

Outguides

Outguides can be inserted into the system when a file is removed. These help to keep a record of the location of files when they are not in the system. The outguides should be inserted in the system in place of the files, and should record file, date and signature. Outguides are particularly important if the speedy location of files is necessary.

Revision

Revision in necessary to make provision for new topics, changes in activities and new organisations. Revision may take the form of regulating old files, as well as introducing new files.

File creation needs to be flexible but controlled. Allocate responsibility for managing the records management system. Make quick decisions on new files. Tell anybody who needs to know about any amendments. At intervals, say six monthly or annually, review the state of the filing system and overhaul the system.

Group and personal filing

The extent to which files are shared by groups of people needs more attention in the larger organisation, but may still require some thought in the small business. Some documents may be suitable for central filing, while others may be confidential or may only be needed by one person. Whichever system is adopted, staff should have easy access to those files that they use regularly.

Some centralisation of the filing system gives management better control of records. Standardised filing practices can be adopted and staff who are more conversant with records management can take responsibility for the system. On the other hand, centralisation runs the risk of making records less accessible, and delays in accessing files are not uncommon in centralised filing systems. In a small business, centralisation is not likely to be a major issue, but even here it may be necessary to distinguish between personal files and those of the business as a whole, which may be accessed by other staff.

Manuals and codes of practice

A filing system that is likely to persist over a number of years will be used by a variety of different people as staff change. The system should not only be straightforward but also be supported by a manual or code of practice. Such a manual introduces new staff to the system and serves as a reminder to existing staff. It also forms a basis for later decisions on the development of the system and provides some continuity. A manual should outline:

- the purpose of the system
- the basic arrangement of the files, together with codes, if appropriate
- the filing rules used
- security arrangements
- retention policies.

Training

All staff who use the records management system should receive relevant training in filing or retrieval as part of their induction to the organisation. This training will normally be conducted on an individual basis, and bad habits will be passed down with good, so it is important that existing staff understand the system before they are let loose on new recruits.

Some hints

- Work out a mechanism for the collection of papers for filing.
- Index documents, code if necessary, and generate any cross references.
- Sort papers into heaps and then into order.
- Remove paper clips and staples as necessary.
- Keep documents in each folder in date order, with new material at the front.
- Place papers squarely in file. This is tidy and does not hide file tabs.
- Do not remove individual papers from a file.

- Establish a security policy for locking cabinets when you go home in the evening.
- Adopt a routine for conducting filing once a day, such as first thing in the morning.
- Correspondence files are easier to maintain if filing codes are allocated to outgoing mail when letters are typed.

Summary

This chapter offers advice both on how to get a filing system started and how to maintain adequate records. Effective record-keeping is essential to a successful business and is one of the key functions of an office. Although responsibility for the day-to-day maintenance of a records management system can be relegated to office staff, the manager needs to be aware of the options of record-keeping, and if a sound system is in operation, should be able to retrieve any documents from the system in an emergency.

7

Bookkeeping, Budgets, Salaries and VAT

The importance of financial record-keeping

In common with many other office activities, bookkeeping and the maintenance of appropriate financial records are important but should not absorb valuable time that could more profitably be used to gain business. Again, the watchword is keep the records in order and attend to them on a regular basis. In so doing, you will save a lot of time and be in better control of your business.

Financial records are central to every business. If you are not actually in business to make money, you will be using money to support your activities. Financial records have two basic functions:

1. To meet legal requirements, in respect of tax and VAT. Taxpayers who wish to object to an Inland Revenue assessment need records to prove any points when appealing to the Commissioners of the Inland Revenue.
2. To allow you to control business finance both on a day-to-day basis, as well as in the longer term, and thus to monitor whether the business is successful, and to identify any problem areas.

Financial record-keeping, accountancy, and financial and business planning have been the subject of many books, some of which are listed on page 154.

142

This chapter offers only a brief overview of the record-keeping and office activities associated with financial control. Attention is focused on record-keeping, not financial decision-making and control, although good record-keeping is a prerequisite to effective control. A sound financial record-keeping system should be established from the start.

Bookkeeping

Many bookkeeping systems exist of differing levels of complexity. Some of the options are outlined below. Choose a system with a level of complexity suitable to the scale of your activities. Whichever system you choose, clear it with your accountant, to check that the records are adequate for their accounting purposes and will not cause more work, and you more associated expense. If you run your accounts yourself, while the business is still small enough for this to be possible, then you will have a much more complete picture of how the business is developing. Handle the records promptly, entering transactions at least weekly but preferably daily. Obtain a receipt for every purchase. Examine any bank statements and compare them with cheque stubs and paying-in books. Receipts must be retained for several years in order to satisfy the tax authorities.

A simple system

If the number of transactions in your business is small, a very simple system may appeal. The following system will work for the one-person business, and is certainly an advance on chaos. Set up four drawers or files labelled:

1. Unpaid invoices – purchases
2. Unpaid invoices – sales
3. Paid invoices – purchases
4. Paid invoices – sales

With these four categories, nothing should go astray, and it is relatively easy to monitor what you owe and what is owed to you.

Simplex or one-entry systems

Simplex or one-entry systems are a relatively straightforward method of bookkeeping, enabling records to be maintained in odd moments during the day and a short period of bookkeeping at the end of the week.

Books can be purchased to support this method of bookkeeping , and they come ready ruled. Although complex at first sight, they in fact assist in easy bookkeeping. Each week has a separate page. Pages have the following sections:

- Receipts
- Paid to bank
- Payments for business stock, eg goods for resale or raw materials
- Payments other than for stock, eg rent, rates or car expenses.

Other sections also cover private pension contributions, PAYE, National Insurance, drawings for self, and capital items.

Books consist of 53 weekly pages, with little carrying forward between pages. At the back of the book, there are three double-pages for entering summaries. These summaries include:

- Summary of weekly takings, which reflect sales
- Payments for expenses
- Drawings for self
- Summary of capital expenses incurred during the year
- Goods taken for own consumption.

Using these pages, it is easy to draw up final accounts, including the Trading Account, the Profit and Loss Account, and the Balance Sheet as described in the next section on double-entry bookkeeping.

Double-entry bookkeeping

Double-entry bookkeeping is the correct way to keep accounts and is widely used in business. As you will appreciate from this brief description, it is relatively complex, so that for the smallest of businesses one of the methods discussed above is more appropriate. However, as the business expands, it will be necessary to consider double-entry bookkeeping. This section introduces the principles of the system and some key jargon. When double-entry bookkeeping becomes advisable, it may be worth attending a training course. Even if a bookkeeper is responsible for maintaining the records, it is important for you to be able to understand them.

The doubly-entry system involves original documents, the books of original entry, ledger entries, the trial balance and the final accounts. These are described below.

Original documents

Every transaction, be it a purchase, sale, or payment, has an original document such as an invoice, credit note or statement.

Books of original entry

The details on the original documents are first entered in a book of original entry or a Day Book. Purchase invoices go in the Purchases Day Book and sales invoices in the Sales Day Book. Day books keep a record of documents received in chronological order.

Ledger

The contents of day books are subsequently posted to the ledger. Every transaction appears twice, both as a debit entry and as a credit entry. For example, where goods for resale are purchased on credit from M. Smith, the transaction is first entered in the Purchases Day Book on receipt of the invoice. In double-entry bookkeeping, this would be transferred to the ledger in the form of a debit entry made in the Purchases Account and a credit entry made in the account of M. Smith. This implies that one account will be kept for each creditor or debtor, and thus tens or hundreds of accounts may be maintained. Total entries on the debit side should balance total entries on the credit side.

Trial balance
After a few weeks, a check is performed to assess whether the ledger entries are accurate. This check is referred to as a trial balance. The trial balance is calculated by adding up all the debit entries and all the credit entries. This is done by first working out a balance for each individual account by totalling each side and adding the difference to the lesser side to make the account balance. When the debit and credit totals do not balance, there must be an error, and this must be located.

Final accounts
The final accounts draw together all financial information, so that it is possible to assess whether the business is making a profit. The final accounts comprise:

- *Trading Account*, which is a summary of the trading position, usually over 12 months. The trading account details stock, purchases and sales figures for the period, and provides the gross profit of trading.
- *Profit and Loss Account*. The gross profit calculated and shown in the Trading Account is carried over to the Profit and Loss Account. Any other profits made from other investments are added to this figure. Items of expenditure incurred in the operation of the business, such as rent, rates and lighting, are offset against profits.
- *Balance Sheet*, which summarises all balances of accounts still remaining in the trial balance after the preparation of the trading, and profit and loss accounts. These remaining accounts represent the assets and liabilities of the business such as cash and bank balances, debtors, creditors, premises, fixtures and fittings, loans and capital invested by the owner.

Computer-based bookkeeping systems

Computer-based bookkeeping systems operate on the same principles as manual bookkeeping systems, but the tedium of manual entries and the transfer of figures from one book to another is eliminated. A supplier's bill that has been paid can be keyed in, and once it has been checked for accuracy, the payment can be recorded, the balance owing to the supplier reduced, the VAT input tax calculated and recorded, and the purchase added to the Purchases Account, and, if necessary, the profit of the business calculated. Computer-based systems may produce a running balance after each transaction, as well as documents such as those that need to be sent to debtors.

The one-entry system described earlier has an equivalent software package, Micro-Simplex. This operates in a similar way to the manual system, but also offers other useful modules, such as an unpaid bills module, an outstanding invoices module, a VAT reporting module, and a stock control module.

Budgets

Budgets are a useful tool for financial control, and provide forecasts of income and expenditure and targets to aim for. Targets (or business plans) take time to prepare and for budgets to be of any value, it is necessary to monitor and measure results against the targets. Monitoring and control can only be achieved with the support of appropriate record-keeping.

Office budgets are likely to relate to: staff salaries, equipment, consumables (such as stationery and office supplies), running costs (such as lighting and heating), rent, rates, and insurance, telephone charges, printing and postage. A budget for the entire business will show planned revenue, capital expenditure, production costs etc. Budgets need to distinguish capital and revenue. They cannot always be met. There may be unpredicted changes in the level and nature of business activity, salaries, and practices, such as those associated with the introduction of computer-based systems. In such cases a revised budget should be prepared, but the results still monitored against the original, so the variance can be measured and corrective action taken in good time. Records associated with meeting budget targets need to monitor expenditure and income against the forecast, and generate feedback into subsequent budgets.

Value added tax

Every business which is VAT registered is responsible for collecting tax on the value added to any goods as they pass through its hands. VAT is administered by HM Customs and Excise. Look them up in the phone book and ask for their free leaflets and any special advice.

Every trader whose *turnover* exceeds £25,400 (1990–91 figure) per annum has to register and keep VAT records. Prior to 1990–91 there was also a quarterly registration limit but this has been abolished. Traders with lower turnovers are not required to register for VAT, but they should consider whether voluntary registration will be beneficial. Only by being registered for VAT can you claim back VAT paid on goods supplied to you. Many businesses pay out a lot of VAT on equipment and stock before sales have been built up to a level where the trader is required to register.

At present there are only two rates of VAT, zero rate (0 per cent) and standard rate at 15 per cent. Goods in neither category are exempt from VAT.

VAT records should record:

- Inputs (purchases)
- Input tax paid
- Outputs (sales)
- Output tax collected

The balance between input tax and output tax collected is normally positive and is due to Customs and Excise. Some retailers who sell mostly zero-rated goods are not collecting tax from their customers, but may be paying tax on inputs. They can therefore claim refunds. VAT records can be divided into two types: normal VAT records, and special schemes for retailers and other suppliers.

Normal VAT records must be kept for all items purchased and supplied where suppliers and traders issue tax invoices.

The Simplex VAT Record Book is widely available, and has columns already ruled. It has pages for input tax and output tax. In the input account are recorded: the invoice total, the cost of taxable goods, and zero-rated goods, and the deductible VAT input tax. Another page records input returns or credits on goods purchased. The totals for the accounting period must show the figure to claim back on the VAT account. Similar pages are ruled for output tax, resulting in the total output tax to be taken into the VAT account.

Retailers, or anyone else who supplies goods and services to the public without tax invoices, cannot calculate the tax on every 'supply' or sale as it takes place and special schemes have been devised which work out the VAT situation based on total takings. These schemes rely upon a strict record being kept of daily takings. At the end of the VAT period a calculation is made to assess how much VAT is due. Details of the schemes, which cater for different kinds of trader, are given in Notice 727: Special Schemes for Retailers.

For most traders a VAT account is rendered at the end of every quarter and the VAT return completed and sent to the VAT Central Unit. For traders dealing with zero-rated items a VAT return is normally sent in monthly in order to recoup tax more speedily.

Record-keeping for VAT may be tedious, but you have a responsibility to keep adequate records and make appropriate payments. The penalities for error or fraudulent evasion can be high, so it is prudent to master VAT as it affects you. VAT staff can be helpful to anyone with a genuine need for guidance.

Wages and Salaries

When wages are paid weekly, the amount is calculated either on an hourly rate, plus overtime paid at a higher rate, or a weekly rate for a defined working week. The pay prior to any deductions is referred to as the gross pay, and the pay after deductions – the net pay – is what the employee receives. Wages are sometimes paid in cash, but increasingly are paid into a bank, post office or building society account. This avoids the security hazards associated with handling large amounts of cash.

Salaries are normally paid monthly and calculated as a proportion of the annual gross salary figure, less deductions, and are usually paid into the employee's account. The employee receives a salary slip giving the following information:

- name
- department and employee number
- tax code number
- annual salary figure
- National Insurance number
- gross salary figure for the period covered
- any additions in respect of back pay, tax refund, overtime payments etc
- statutory deductions, including income tax, superannuation, pension contributions, and National Insurance
- voluntary deductions, such as trade union subscriptions, and covenants

The main statutory deductions are income tax and National Insurance. Income tax is calculated by the employer using tax tables and the employee's tax code, issued by the Inland Revenue. You should keep abreast of changes in tax allowances and tax bands, and changes in the employee's circumstances. The Employer's Guide to PAYE, issued by the Inland Revenue as leaflet IR53, explains the Inland Revenue's viewpoint and gives a chart that explains how to make employee's wage deductions. This leaflet lists five key things that you as the employer are responsible for:

1. Telling the Inland Revenue when an employee starts work
2. Working out tax and National Insurance contributions that are due each pay day
3. Paying these contributions to the Inland Revenue Accounts Office each month
4. Telling the tax office when an employee leaves
5. Telling the tax office at the end of each year how much each employee has earned.

When an employee starts work for the first time the employer deducts tax under the emergency code. The employee needs to complete a coding claim form and send it to the tax office, from whence the employer should then receive a notice of coding. When an employee leaves a given employment, a certificate on form P45 'Particulars of employee leaving' must be prepared. Parts 2 and 3 of the P45 are given to the employee to give to their next employer, and part 1 is returned to the tax office. Any potential employee who has previously been in employment should offer you a P45. After April 5 each year, the employer is required to give a certificate of pay and tax deductions, P60, to each employee. The employer is required to make returns to the Collector of Taxes not later than 19 April each year, showing pay, tax, statutory sick pay, statutory maternity pay and National Insurance contributions of all employees.

National Insurance contributions are related to earnings and are collected under PAYE. Contributions are partly payable by the employee and partly by the employer. Several classes of contribution are available and the one that is appropriate depends on whether the contributor is employed or self-employed. Most people working for an employer are subject to Class 1 contributions. The current National Insurance leaflet is available from post offices, and the Department of Health and Social Security issues another useful leaflet entitled 'Employer's guide to NI Contributions'. Contribution tables are available from the Department of Health and Social Security.

The office will need to maintain a record of wages, salaries, tax, and National Insurance contributions that have been paid. The Simplex Wages Book is one simple device for recording such data.

An employee is eligible for statutory sick pay (SSP) when a period of sickness covers four or more consecutive days, up to a limit of eight weeks in any tax year. Statutory sick pay for this period is payable by the employer. Where the sick period exceeds eight weeks, payment may be made from an employer's sick pay scheme, the State scheme or some other benefit scheme. An employer can get compensation from the Department of Social Security broadly equivalent to his share of National Insurance contributions paid on Statutory Sick Pay.

Employers are responsible for paying statutory maternity pay (SMP) for up to 18 weeks to pregnant women whom they have employed for at least six months before the qualifying week, which is 15 weeks before the baby is due, and who pay National Insurance contributions. The local office of the Department of Social Security will be able to offer advice on National Insurance, statutory sick pay and statutory maternity pay.

Petty cash

A petty cash book is often used in an office for recording small items of business expenditure. The best known method for operating petty cash is the imprest system. The three stages of the imprest system are:

1. The person responsible for petty cash is allocated a sum of money sufficient to cover a month's outgoings on minor items.
2. During the month, this money is used for paying for small purchases.
3. At the end of the month the petty cash is made up to the original amount.

Whenever cash is paid out, a voucher or receipt is obtained. These vouchers can be numbered as they are received and filed in numerical order. The petty cash book removes many small items from the Purchases Day Book. The amount credited to the petty cash book needs to be shown in the Purchases Day Book and the Ledger.

Summary

This chapter has briefly reviewed some of the record-keeping associated with exercising financial control over a small business.

Further Reading from Kogan Page

Chapter 1: The Office and its Environment

Fit for Work: A Practical Guide to Good Health for People Who Sit on the Job, Scott W Donkin, 1990

How to Choose Business Premises, H Green, B Chalkley and P Foley, 1986

A Manager's Guide toHealth and Safety at Work, Jeremy Stranks, 1990

Chapter 2: Office Personnel

Effective Interviewing, John Fletcher, 1988

Employment Law for the Small Business, Anne Knell, 1989

How to Write a Staff Manual, S L Brock and S R Cabbell, 1990

Readymade Interview Questions, Malcolm Peel, 1989

Readymade Job Advertisements: A Recruitment Toolkit for Every Manager, Neil Wenborn, 1991

Chapter 3: Office Equipment and Supplies

Buying for Business, Tony Attwood, 1988

Running Your Own Word Processing Service, 2nd Edition, Doreen Huntley, 1991

Chapter 4: The Electronic Office

So You Think Your Business Needs a Computer? Khalid Aziz, 1986

Chapter 5: Communication and the Office

Distribution for the Small Business, Nicholas Mohr, 1990
Effective Meeting Skills, Marion E Haynes, 1988
How to Make Meetings Work, Malcolm Peel, 1988
Improving Your Communication Skills, Malcolm Peel, 1990

Chapter 7: Bookkeeping, Budgets, Salaries and VAT

Do Your Own Bookkeeping, Max Pullen, 1988
Financial Management for the Small Business, 2nd edition, Colin Barrow, 1988
How to Set Up and Run a Payroll System, Carol Anderson, 1990
PAYE, 2nd Edition, Carol Anderson, 1990
VAT and the Small Business, Edmund Tirbutt, 1990
The Stoy Hayward Business Tax Guide, Mavis Seymour and Stephen Say, annual

General

A Handbook of Management Technology, Michael Armstrong, 1988
How to Cut Your Business Costs, Peter D Brunt, 1988
Law for the Small Business, 7th edition, Patricia Clayton, 1991
Starting a Successful Small Business, 2nd edition, M J Morris, 1989

Index